PSYCH FIGHT

An Alternative Perspective on Golf Psychology

JASON BURSTYN

Printed and bound in the United States of America.

ISBN: 978-0-578-62843-1

DEDICATION

To my parents: Thank you for all the support over the years. You have always been encouraging in all my ventures in life. For this, I love and thank you.

I also dedicate this book to anyone who has struggled with golf performance issues similar to mine. You are not alone, I promise you that.

TABLE OF CONTENTS

PREFACE

In life when people reach a certain amount of prominence, others tend to believe what these individuals say at face value. We don't question their theories, advice, or facts, because they have achieved a certain level of expertise or stature in their respective field. However, with other facets in life, most people want to know as much information as possible and do not easily accept what they are told. When someone is about to embark on a large purchase, they will ask others with a similar product if they have had a good experience with it, if it's safe, durable, and go through an extensive information gathering process. A consumer generally has a degree of skepticism when a salesman tries to sell them a product, and to relieve that feeling they will inquire about the pricing, warranties, and other details in an effort to feel comfortable with the purchase they are about to make.

Similarly, many golf psychologists have been validated in golf society by players, commentators, and casual fans to the point where they have reached a certain level of prominence and as a result golfers have lost their skepticism about the information these individuals put forth and accept what they say without any hesitation. This is the heart of my story, the inspiration for writing this tale. As a talented golfer whose journey began at the age of ten, there was always a constant roadblock to my game: the mental aspect. Despite these mental roadblocks, a successful junior and college golf career were achieved. As a result, upon graduating from college, I chased my dream of trying to make it to the PGA Tour in pursuit of fortune and fame. Ultimately, my mind held me back.

I knew my mind was the biggest pitfall of my game, thus throughout my golf journey, I sought the help of numerous prominent experts in the field of golf psychology. Unfortunately, I was someone who blindly accepted the sayings and clichés of golf psychologists and did not do my due diligence of questioning the information that was presented to me. In the end the information that was presented to me by these experts did not provide any lasting solutions, just more confusion, frustration, and time wasted. Due to my lack of results with the golf psychology field, I felt the need to write this story in an effort to share with the golfing world a different perspective about golf psychology aside from blind acceptance.

CHAPTER 1

Psych 101

Zeitgeist: a German word meaning "spirit of the times." It is a concept that refers to the dominant set of ideals and beliefs of a particular time in history. It encompasses the collective thought patterns of groups which dictate what is trendy or acceptable. These generally accepted schools of thought motivate the actions of members of society during that time. One zeitgeist throughout history has been that the world is flat, which instilled fear in explorers that they would fall off the earth. The zeitgeist in Salem, Massachusetts, was that some women were witches, leading to mass hysteria, confusion, and loss of life for many innocent women. When women felt nervous or emotional in the nineteenth century, the zeitgeist of the day was that their "wombs were wandering" and they were suffering from female hysteria. Last, but certainly not least, the practice of foot binding was seen as a sign of beauty and elegance in China and practiced for hundreds of years, mostly by upper class women.

The trend that I will be discussing is how sports psychology has become validated in the sport of golf. The masses have flocked to mental "experts" and "gurus" in order to gain a potential competitive edge or to have their minds work as efficiently as possible. Many believe it is essential to have a mental coach or incorporate mental training in order to become the best possible golfer. It has come to the point where many serious golfers believe they must have a sports psychologist to consult with. If they do not, they may feel that they are missing a valuable resource. In recent decades this industry has been validated because a number of successful golfers have consulted with people in this profession.

Before I delve into my personal opinion of golf psychology, I would like to touch briefly on the origins of the field of psychology. Historians argue that there are different starting points to the field. For example, the publishing of Gustav Theodor Fechner's *Elements of* Psychophysics— which demonstrated how to make precise measurements of certain mental quantities—can be seen as one starting point. Others might say psychology started in the seventeenth century when Rene Descartes chose to base his arguments on logic and reasoning and encouraged people to ground their ideas in individual experience instead of authority or tradition.

However, it can be argued that the origins of psychology go much further back. The Greeks engaged intensively in epistemological[1] inquiry. The Greeks' main philosophical question was, "How can we know?" The Sophists[2] of the fifth to second century B.C.E., including Socrates, concerned themselves with this dilemma. Their argument to this perplexing question was that we can never be sure that we know anything because what is the criteria of validity for any

---

[1] Epistemology is the theory of knowledge; it is the investigation of what distinguishes justified belief from opinion.

[2] In ancient Greece, sophism was practiced by the Sophists, a group of teachers of philosophy and rhetoric.

statement? What is considered right or wrong, true or false, good or bad? They all have independent arbitrary points of reference, assumptions, or premises and we can never be certain their points of reference are actually valid.

Now let's fast forward to the late nineteenth century, which many consider to be the official beginning of the study of psychology. Europe, and more specifically Germany, was the epicenter. Some historians consider Wilhelm Wundt to be the father of psychology and 1879 the year it started as this is when Wundt made a formal request to the University of Leipzig to fund an experimental psychology laboratory.

Since Wundt is considered the father of psychology, I will give him a little more air time. According to Wundt the methods of psychology are experimentation and observation. Wundt's form of experimentation was very systematic. He believed that for an experiment to be valid it needed to be repeated systematically with variation of an independent variable, while holding all other conditions constant. From this, an assessment of the changes of a dependent variable could be analyzed. Wundt argued that "higher mental processes," such as emotions, thinking, etc., can only be dealt with by observation which are inaccessible to experimentation. In order to gain knowledge of the higher mental processes he believed in the method of introspection, where subjects were asked to self-examine their own experiences, conscious thoughts, and feelings. In addition, he classified psychology as a topic where subjectivity is left in, whereas other sciences, such as physics, study experience in which subjective matters are removed. The method of introspection is still used today, and yet it is extremely subjective as it is not directly observable and cannot be accurately measured by any metric.

That is all I want to dive into in regards to the history of general psychology. There are plenty of other notable figures, theories, and discoveries that have influenced the field, but I am not trying to put you to sleep by page two.

Now that I have touched on the history of psychology, I am going to give a synopsis of the origins of sports psychology. The name that most frequents as the start of sports psychology is Norman Triplett from the University of Indiana. In an experiment in 1898, he found that cyclists who rode with others performed better. His conclusion was that this was due to the competitive and social aspects of group training that led to improved performance as opposed to simply racing against the clock.

The field lost momentum for about twenty-five years before Coleman Griffith founded the first American sports psychology lab[3] at the University of Illinois in 1925. He worked closely with the football team at Illinois, studying how factors such as psychomotor skills and personality variables related to performance. Due to a lack of interest and funding, the lab closed in 1932, and Griffith was subsequently hired by the Chicago Cubs in 1937.

In 1927, a group at Stanford, consisting of a psychologist Walter Miles, graduate student B.C. Graves, and football coach Glen "Pop" Warner, were interested in finding the fastest way to have an offensive line move in unison. They wanted to see which types of auditory signals were best to quicken the offensive line's reaction time. In order to measure this, Miles invented the "multiple chronograph" capable of simultaneously testing the individual reaction times of seven linemen. Some conclusions that came from this study were that signals called at faster cadences were better for anticipatory signals, whereas slower

---

[3] The first sports psychology lab was founded in Germany by Carl Diem in 1920.

cadences were better for non-anticipatory signals—meaning that the offensive line's speed off the ball was maximized when the quarterback gave signals at those speeds. Although other conclusions were drawn from this experiment, it was overall an advanced experiment that allowed the experimenters to gather quantifiable numbers to reaction times and test multiple variables.

There were other influential figures in sports psychology outside of America. One major contributor was a Russian scholar, Avksentry Cezarevich Puni, from Lesgaft Institute. In one of his writings, *Psychological Preparation of Athletes for a Competition,* he states that the psychological preparation of the athlete is considered necessary for successful performance in competitions. Additionally, if the psychological aspects of sports training are ignored, this can lead to unfavorable consequences. He stated that this problem is far from being completely understood from a practical and theoretical standpoint. Puni strongly believed that athletes should be independent of their coaches in order to make the right decisions in competition.[4] Moreover, psychological preparation for a competition must be individualized, meaning it must be based on the peculiarities of that specific athlete. All of these individual attributes, such as temperament, character, and motivation, must be considered in order to best identify the appropriate techniques of psychological preparation for the athlete. Puni did have other beliefs, such as goal setting and classifying events into varying degrees of importance, and is considered as one of the earliest contributing figures to sports psychology.

I don't want this book to be a boring history lesson on psychology, but I felt it was important to give some background of the science

---

[4] These were very radical beliefs as they were against communist ideals; Puni, however, was not a member of the communist party.

and its origins. I will sporadically reference these people and their theories later in the book, so this also serves as a glossary of sorts.

Now onto the good stuff. The real purpose of the book: GOLF PSYCHOLOGY. I don't really know when golf psychology originated or when it really became popular, but I know that the most prominent and influential figure of the field is Dr. Bob Rotella, from the University of Virginia. He has worked with many PGA Tour pros and really popularized the profession. I will compliment him and say that he marketed himself well and got the necessary clientele so that he became the "guy" for golf psychology. If you want a private session for two days with him, it will cost you upwards of $5,000—not bad for two days' work. If I had to guess a lot of psychologists essentially followed the path that Rotella paved and flooded the golf scene.

So what do you think my opinion of golf psychology is? Is the suspense killing you? Well, here it is. I am here to argue that golf psychology is not legitimate. To put it very broadly, golf psychology lacks evidence. The biggest issue that I have with golf psychologists is that they make it seem that their theories are proven or are fact. Of the golf psychology books that I have read, psychologists do not put forth much effort into trying to back up their theories with noteworthy evidence, such as referencing studies, statistics, or anything along those lines. Psychology in and of itself is a very subjective field, and consequently, golf psychologists struggle to provide sufficient answers when they attempt to prove their points. In fact, all matters of the mind, character, soul, or whatever you want to call it, have a degree of mysticism to them. There are so many factors that influence who we are, what we perceive as stress, opportunity, fear, joy, and other emotional characteristics.

Despite not being able to provide evidence to back up their statements, golf shrinks make it seem like their theories are fact and you are performing a disservice to yourself if you don't listen to them. In addition, they make it sound like the panacea for everyone's mental issues is to simply follow their cookie-cutter methods. For a vast majority of the topics they discuss, the only evidence they provide is purely anecdotal evidence that relies on personal testimony. Essentially it is "he said/she said" evidence; the personal testimony that shrinks acquire is from PGA Tour players. Basically, the only validation of their theories is that their clients use their methods. Throughout this book, however, I will demonstrate that this is insufficient as there is plenty of anecdotal evidence that contradicts what they say. At the very least, I will provide a tie in arguments based on the counterevidence. In addition, I will provide my personal rationalization of different golf psychology topics and hope that my logic and reasoning will persuade the reader of my perspective.

Because of the inherent subjectivity of sports psychology and psychology as a whole, I am a very firm believer in the following statement—**"there is no right or wrong"**—when it comes to the mental side of golf. Golfers should do what works for them in terms of a mental approach despite what any "golf psychologist," "mental guru," or "expert" says is right or wrong. Going back to the ancient Greek philosophers, they stated that it is fundamentally impossible to know whether something is right or wrong because thoughts and feelings do not happen in a perfect vacuum, thus it is nearly impossible to replicate these points of reference and make sound conclusions. In other words, psychology is a field where the waters are very murky and it is nearly impossible to pinpoint why certain psychological phenomena happen. They are produced by many factors that can occur at different levels of explanation. Furthermore, these causes might not be independent of one another, they can be associated such that when one factor is present other factors may or may not be present as well. This overlap, or lack thereof, makes it nearly impossible to pinpoint the causation(s) of certain psychological events. Because of this mysticism, Plato believed that "the self" is the only object that one can learn about with any degree of assurance. Socrates has been attributed with saying, "To know thyself is the beginning of wisdom"—very wise words from one of the founding fathers of Western philosophy. I subscribe to Socrates's school of thought of "knowing thyself." This is my argument and suggestion to every golfer out there: "know thyself." Although I also like to say **there is no right or wrong**.

Golf psychologists have created a standardized approach that they believe will work for everybody—a one-size-fits-all approach. This is the opposite of what Puni suggested: that every athlete is an individual, and therefore they should figure out what works best for them. This is the school of thought I subscribe to.

As you continue to read you will get insights into my motivations as to why I am so passionate about the subject. Additionally, I will cover other topics such as my issues with golf commentators, golf culture, generally accepted schools of thought, and my two cents on professional golf. But the main goal of this book is to challenge the zeitgeist of the validity and necessity of golf psychology. At the very least, I hope to provide you with a new perspective, food for thought, and a heavy dose of skepticism about the industry.

CHAPTER 2

My Golf Career

I was born on October 29, 1989, in Miami, Florida. Both my maternal and paternal grandparents are from Eastern Europe and were victims of Nazi Germany's takeover of Europe. They were all sent to labor camps and escaped. My father's parents hid in the forests of Poland and my mother's parents joined the Partisans in Poland, a resistance group that fought the Germans. After the war, they lived in displaced persons' camps for about five years before immigrating to America in the late 1940s. My maternal grandparents settled in Bayonne, New Jersey. When my mom's father lived in Poland he was a bookkeeper. When they moved to Jersey, they opened up a general clothing store on the first floor of the small two-story house they lived in. My maternal grandfather became a foreman at the Manischewitz Matzoh factory. That is how they made a living. They worked extremely hard and were able to send my mom to medical school and my aunt to law school. My paternal grandparents moved to Sharon, Massachusetts. My paternal grandfather built manholes and septic tanks when he lived in Europe. When they moved to Massachusetts, he first worked in a butcher shop and bought a chicken farm with his savings. He then used his savings from the chicken farm to start his own construction company, eventually doing the same work in America as he had in Europe. He was responsible for installing some of the original sewer systems in Boston from the 1960s to 1980s. He was able to provide for his wife and three kids and send all of his kids to college, including law school for my father.

My mother and father both went to the University of Miami (UM) for their respective advanced degrees. My mother for medical school (1980s) and my father for law school (1970s). They met at a sports club and my father proposed to my mom after dating for only six weeks. I am the younger of two sons. My father is a personal injury attorney and my mother has been a pathologist at the University of Miami for over thirty years.

"You have to play a sport every single year"—this was a house rule and what I remember my father saying. As a result, growing up I played many sports. For the most part, I was a natural when it came to sports. I was a great catcher and hitter in little league baseball and made the all-star team when I was in third grade. I played center and defensive line in Pop Warner football, as well as played the whole game on both sides of the ball. At the end of the year ceremony, the coaches handed out four footballs to the most valuable players of the team. After the first three were given out and I had not received one, the whole team started chanting "Jason, Jason, Jason." And guess what? I didn't get that football! The coach's son got it. That happened in 1998 and to this day it still chaps my ass. Don't worry this book will not be a tale of how great I am or glorifying myself; there will be plenty of honesty in it.

It was around the age of nine when I started to play golf and tennis. I do not remember initially being obsessed with golf and having it take over my life from the get go. It was just another sport I was playing. However, I started playing it more and more around that time since I injured my Achilles heel and could not play tennis for about three weeks. My father got me set up with some golf lessons with a professional at a golf course in Miami. My first instructor was one of the most energetic and passionate people I have ever met. He really got me enthused and excited about golf. When I first started playing golf, I struggled and would shoot in the 100s, but I progressed quickly. I began playing in tournaments shortly after starting and began to shoot good scores. I think within one year I competed in the Optimist International in West Palm Beach and came in third place, shooting scores of 69-71 from the red tees. In addition, I came in second in the National Putt Pitch and Drive in 1999, which took place at the Magnolia Golf Course in Walt Disney World. Of course, now the kids do the finals at Augusta National—lucky bastards!

But allow me to backtrack, I am going to highlight some of my golfing accomplishments throughout my career and some tournaments where there were recognizable names. My father has cataloged my entire golf career since the day it started. There is essentially a library full of my tournament results from day one—which is where I got the following information. When I first started to play golf, I sent my swing to the Golf Channel and got selected to be on Academy Live. On the following page is the fax. I was nine years old and, if I may say so, I think I did a great job on that show. I wore my red shirt, pants, and chain-link necklace, which happened to be the only outfit I ever wore when I was a little kid.

THE GOLF CHANNEL

June 10,1999

Mr. David Burstyn
Fax: 305/371-9603

Dear Mr. Burstyn,

Thank you for helping me get your son, Jason on *Academy Live* on June 23rd. Enclosed you will find directions to The Golf Channel.

Basically all we need is for you and Jason to be at The Golf Channel no later than 6:30 p.m. The show begins at 8 p.m. and lasts for an hour. I also need him to wear dark colors. Dark blues, green, red, anything solid will show up best on television. If you have a question pertaining to this, definitely give me a call. My phone number is (407)248-3311.

We're excited to have Jason on the show. We will have our instructors look at his swing and he will help us answer questions from our junior callers. When you do arrive at The Golf Channel, just ask for me and I'll bring the both of you to the studio to meet Peter Kessler and the guest instructor, Jane Frost.

Please have a safe trip to Orlando and we'll see you on the 23rd.

Sincerely,

Danielle Williams
Production Coordinator, *Academy Live*

I will highlight scores from some of the first tournaments I ever played to show that I did not at first excel. They were part of a series called the Dade Amateur Golf Association. I averaged roughly 50 for nine holes in five nine-hole events during the summer of 1999. I won all of these little tournaments, except for one, but that is not my point. The point is that averaging 50 for nine holes is pretty terrible. But, as I said, I quickly improved.

When I was ten years old, I played in the 1999 Doral Publix and came in fifteenth place. Recognize who came in fourth, fifth, and twenty-sixth place? Hopefully you all know who the guy in fourth place is, but Scott Pinckney was a member of the PGA Tour and Tony Finau is one of the best players on the planet now. I actually played my first nine holes with Tony that tournament. He must have been a foot taller than me and he bombed the ball back then.

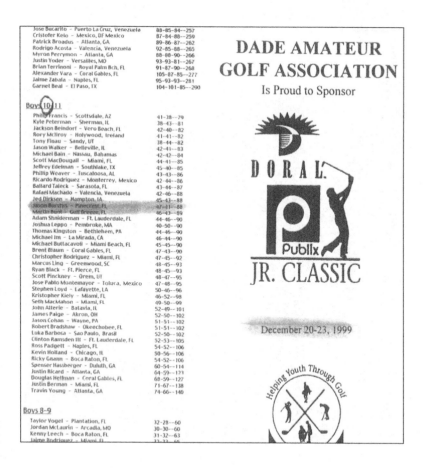

Jose Bucarito - Puerto La Cruz, Venezuela   88-85-84--257
Cristofer Kelo - Mexico, DF Mexico   87-84-88--259
Patrick Broadus - Atlanta, GA   89-86-87--262
Rodrigo Acosta - Valencia, Venezuela   92-85-88--265
Myron Perrymon - Atlanta, GA   88-88-90--266
Justin Yoder - Versailles, MO   93-93-81--267
Brian Terrinoni - Royal Palm Bch, FL   91-87-90--268
Alexander Vara - Coral Gables, FL   105-87-85--277
Jaime Zabala - Naples, FL   95-93-93--281
Garnet Beal - El Paso, TX   104-101-85--290

Boys 10-11

Philip Francis - Scottsdale, AZ   41-38--79
Kyle Peterman - Sherman, IL   38-43--81
Jackson Beindorf - Vero Beach, FL   42-40--82
Rory McIlroy - Holywood, Ireland   41-41--82
Tony Finau - Sandy, UT   38-44--82
Jason Walker - Belleville, IL   42-41--83
Michael Bain - Nassau, Bahamas   42-42--84
Scott MacDougall - Miami, FL   44-41--85
Jeffrey Edelman - Southlake, TX   45-40--85
Phillip Weaver - Tuscaloosa, AL   43-43--86
Ricardo Rodriguez - Monterrey, Mexico   42-44--86
Ballard Taleck - Sarasota, FL   43-44--87
Rafael Machado - Valencia, Venezuela   42-46--88
Jed Dirksen - Hampton, IA   45-43--88
Jason Burstyn - Pinecrest, FL   47-41--88
Martin Bunt - Gulf Breeze, FL   46-43--89
Adam Shniderman - Ft. Lauderdale, FL   44-46--90
Joshua Leppo - Pembroke, MA   40-50--90
Thomas Kingston - Bethlehem, PA   44-46--90
Michael Im - La Mirada, CA   46-44--90
Michael Buttacavoli - Miami Beach, FL   45-45--90
Brent Blaum - Coral Gables, FL   47-43--90
Christopher Rodriguez - Miami, FL   47-45--92
Marcus Ling - Greenwood, SC   48-45--93
Ryan Black - Ft. Pierce, FL   48-45--93
Scott Pinckney - Orem, UT   48-47--95
Jose Pablo Montemayor - Toluca, Mexico   47-48--95
Stephen Loyd - Lafayette, LA   50-46--96
Kristopher Kiely - Miami, FL   46-52--98
Seth MacMahon - Miami, FL   49-50--99
John Alterie - Batavia, IL   52-49--101
James Paige - Akron, OH   52-50--102
Jason Cohan - Wayne, PA   51-51--102
Robert Bradshaw - Okeechobee, FL   51-51--102
Luka Barbosa - Sao Paulo, Brasil   52-50--102
Clinton Ramsden III - Ft. Lauderdale, FL   52-53--105
Ross Padgett - Naples, FL   54-52--106
Kevin Holland - Chicago, IL   50-56--106
Ricky Gnann - Boca Raton, FL   54-52--106
Spenser Hassberger - Duluth, GA   60-54--114
Justin Ricard - Atlanta, GA   64-59--123
Douglas Helfman - Coral Gables, FL   68-59--127
Justin Berman - Miami, FL   71-67--138
Travin Young - Atlanta, GA   74-66--140

Boys 8-9

Taylor Vogel - Plantation, FL   32-28--60
Jordan McLaurin - Arcadia, MO   30-30--60
Kenny Leech - Boca Raton, FL   31-32--63
Jaime Rodriguez - Miami, FL   32-33--65

DADE AMATEUR GOLF ASSOCIATION

Is Proud to Sponsor

DORAL.

Publix

JR. CLASSIC

December 20-23, 1999

Helping Youth Through Golf

In August 2000, I played in the World Junior Masters in Hawaii and came in eighth place. Here is a picture from the tournament. Tony Finau won the tournament; he is next to Chi Chi. Opposite of Tony in the same row is Rory Mcilroy. I am in the center of the front row.

A few weeks later I played in a tournament on the Okeeheelee Junior Golf Tour (OJGF) where they had one day events. I shot 62 for thirteen holes. Recognize who I beat that day who shot 63? I think Brooks gets the last laugh though, he is certainly a hell of a lot richer, more famous, and better at golf than me.

2000 OJGF/PGA Championship- August 26th

Okeeheelee Golf Course, West Palm Beach, FL

Boys 14 & Up Divisions
Boys Championship-18 holes
Beau Deason* 71
Pete Vilairatana 71
Willy Gray 80
Mike Zurek 83
Mike Carpenter 83
Tripp Robb 84
Corey Henry 85
Boys 14 & Up -1st Flight
Greg Gonzales 76
Eric Metzker 78
Matt Herman 79
Schuyler Michael 80
Mike Stango 81
Matt Doughty 81
Aaron Gordon 83
Chad Lubart 84
Mike Prince 85
Teddy Romfh 87
Devin Kanhai 88
Mike Politis 89
Braden List 90
Jeb Geesey 92
Tim McArthur 94
Shawn Gruber 94
Kamron Hays 95
Brian Birney 96
Kenny Gray 102

Boys 12-13-13 holes
Kevin Steakin 76
Kodi Merrell 79
Jason Walker 80
Brian Terrinoni 82
Robbie Wight 82
Alexander Vara 83
Tony Park 85
Danny Divito 86
Danny Gervasio 87
Dustin Doran 87
Mike Freemen 90
Ryan LeFevre 90
Eric Chaves 91
Matt Applebaum 91
Chris Kushay 96
Jimmy Lytle 96
BJ Price 102
Martin Folker 103
Matt Tubbs 125
Nick Spear 132

Boys 10-11-13 holes
Matt Scarlett 52
Jack Beindorf 53
Mike Weir 58
Graham Bradshaw 60
Jhared Hack 60
Kenny Leech 61
Jason Burstyn 62
Brooks Koepka 63
Gabriel Costa 63
Clint Ramsden 64
Chris Crawford 65
Ricky Gnann 67
Jake Gabel 69
Alex Yost 71
Chris Rodriguez 74
Blaine West 76
Max Murray 76
Daniel Candon 79
Chip Wight 88
Josh Reich 94
Stephen Bradford 100

Boys 8-9- 9 holes
Taylor Vogel 36
Lawrence Renouf 39
Robby Chiste 42

In December 2000, I played again in the Doral Publix. Here are the results from that year. You should recognize quite a few names here as well. Looks like I got the better of Patrick Reed at this tournament, but he definitely gets the last laugh.

Boys 10-11

Martin Buhl - Gulf Breeze, FL	35-35--70
Eduardo Perez - Quito, Ecuador	36-36--72
Peter Uhlein - Dartmouth, MA	36-37--73
Tony Finau - Sandy, VT	37-37--74
Rory McIlroy - Holywood, CD	36-40--76
Scott Kelly - Houston, TX	38-38--76
Jhared Hack - Longwood, FL	41-36--77
Gipper Finau - Sandy, VT	39-38--77
James Byrd - Longwood, FL	39-38--77
Scott Spiewak - Prescott, AZ	39-39--78
Ramsay Quinn - Wilmington, NC	42-37--79
Kyle Cothran - Chattanooga, TN	39-40--79
Jackson Beindorf - Vero Beach, FL	37-42--79
Scott Pinckney - Orem, UT	38-42--80
Johnny Widmer - Grand Cayman, Cayman Island	44-37--81
Eugenio Garza - Mexico City, Mexico	39-42--81
Jose Farias - Monterrey, NL Mexico	40-42--82
Justin Dorward - Port St. Lucie, FL	41-41--82
Esteban Aristizabal - Medellin, Colombia	40-42--82
Scott MacDougall - Miami, FL Bahamas	42-41--83
Kenny Leech - Boca Raton, FL	43-40--83
Andrew Glassell - Clarksville, TN	41-42--83
Samuel Braver - Alpharetta, GA	43-40--83
Jason Burstyn - Miami, FL	43-41--84
Patrick Reed - San Antonio, TX	41-44--85
Robert Bradshaw - Ft. Pierce, FL	46-40--86
Caio Barbosa - Sao Paulo, Brasil	41-45--86
Felipe Velazquez - Caracas, Venezuela	43-44--87
Jordan McLaurin - Arcadia, MO	44-43--87
Julian Jimenez - San Jose, Costa Rica	43-44--87
Kenji Manuel Hernandez - Alizeaan Zarago, Me	42-45--87
Ford Fischer - Dallas, TX	44-43--87
Preston Knox - Dunedin, FL	41-47--88
Brett Falkoff - Lafayette Hill, PA	42-46--88
Diego Castilla - Laredo, TX	42-46--88
Jon Alterie - Batavia, IL	44-44--88
Tommy Gibson - Wilmington, NC	47-42--89
Ryan Black - Ft Pierce, FL	44-45--89
Rafael Gomez - Lerma, Mexico	46-44--90
Daniel Condelio - Longwood, FL	48-42--90
Ross Padgett - Naples, FL	48-43--91
Paul Josephs - Vero Beach, FL	45-46--91
Jorge Alvarez - Garza Garcia, NL Mexico	45-46--91
Diego Acosta - Valencia, Venezuela	47-44--91
P Wasserman - Chepachet, RI	50-42--92
Justin Ricard - Atlanta, GA	47-45--92
Jacob Gabel - Boca Raton, FL	49-43--92
Marcello Gauss - Sao Paulo, Brazil	51-42--93
Chase Ferris - Flushing, MI	50-43--93
Nicholas Santora - Naples, FL	47-47--94
Jason Cohan - Wayne, PA	46-48--94
Andrew Clarke - Plantation, FL	51-43--94
Daniel Candon - Surfside, FL	49-45--94
Joshua Seale - Orlando, FL	47-49--96
Jackson Eggers - Atlanta, GA	50-47--97
Hayes Brown - Atlanta, GA	50-47--97
Jason Anderson - Plantation, FL	48-50--98
Christopher Carlin - Pembroke Pines, FL	51-48--99
Gary Quinn - Anthem, AZ	56-45--101
Johnny Hayes - Cape Elizabeth, ME	50-51--101
Joseph Anderson - Plantation, FL	47-57--104
Frank Rodriquez - Coral Gables, FL	52-58--110
Geoffrey Gilbert - Coral Gables, FL	62-57--119
Christian Brand - Hialeah, FL	61-59--120
Doug Hellman - Coral Gables, FL	63-65--128
Kristian McSweeney - Nassau, Bahamas	69-67--136
Bryan Saul - Coral Gables, FL	83-67--150
Justin Berman - Miami, FL	68-68 --WD

Boys 8-9

Taylor Vogel - Plantation, FL	26-30--56
Roberto Machado - Miami, FL	34-30--64
David Dewey - Garza Garcia, NL Mexico	33-31--64
Blake Biddle - St. Charles, IL	33-32--65
Alex Weiss - Sherman Oaks, CA	32-34--66
Lawrence Renouf - Miami, FL	34-32--66
Curtis Thompson - Coral Springs, FL	35-32--67
Jaime Rodriquez - Miami, FL	31-36--67
James David - Miami, FL	32-35--67
Michael Chipolone - Parkland, F	34-33--67
Jan Vincent Jaro - Jacksonville, FL	33-35--68
Daniel Perez Oquendo - Punta DeMata, Venezue	29-40--69
Gabriel Meares - Laredo, TX Mexico	36-33--69
Ian McConnell - Riverview, FL	33-37--70
Harry Stephenson - Naples, FL	37-35--72
Andres Farias - Monterrey, Mexico	34-38--72
Richard Meier - Coral Springs, FL	40-33--73
Sean Jacklin - Bradenton, FL	36-37--73
James Kim - Miami, FL	37-37--74
Nicholas Torrance - East Lyme, CT	41-34--75
G Stephenson - Naples, FL	40-39--79

DADE AMATEUR GOLF ASSOCIATION

Is Proud to Sponsor

DORAL

Publix

JR. CLASSIC

DECEMBER 20-23, 2000

Helping Youth Through Golf

DAGA

DADE AMATEUR GOLF ASSOCIATION

Girls 16-18 Cha

Niloufar Azam - S
Perry Swenson -
Kelly Husted - Sa
Carmen Alonso -
Jessica Castle -
Lisa Tyler - Light
Maria Martinez -
Tina Miller - Miam
Carolina Llano - M
Paula Creamer -
Ouliana Rotmistrov
Natalia Nicholls -
Erica Battie - Col
Leslie Wall - Dalla
Audrey Gale - Cla
Alessandra Perez
Devan Andersen -
Natascha Lorenz -
Nicole Hage - Cor
Jessica Buchta -

Girls 16-18 Cor

Ali Kicklighter - D
Haley Gildea - Ea
Beth Irwin - Germ
Jillian Burtt - Wet
Lydia Sampson -
Maria Gonzalez -
Courtney Clark -
Elly Leonard - Zio
Kelsey Lutz - Wa
Allison Bourne-Van
Jennifer Ackerson
Analia Lemus - M
Joni Gossett - Ge
Jaclyn Stelzer - A
Veronica Pinel - N
Kristina Prestipino
Nikeda Cooks - L
Marianela Munoz
Brittany Adams -
Tyler Johnson - Pe
Tiffany Woods - E
Michelle Williams
Santie Koch - Po
Britany Wagener -

Girls 14-15

Kelly Froelich - R
Cristie Reed - Co
Emma Cabrera-Bel
Julieta Granada -
Seema Sadokar -
Alejandra Diaz-Cal
Catalina Marin - E
Monique Gesualdi
Maria Germino -
Veronica Felibert
Kelly Robb - Cond
Kelley Leuth - Vic
Whitney Sylvan -
Vanessa Vela - W
Theresa Paik - Si
Mary Calderon - C
Vanessa Brockett
Sands MacDougall
Lauren Mielbrecht
Samantha Widmer

Girls 12-13

Taylor Leon - De
Jennifer Hong - W
Morgan Pressel -
Maria Yacaman -
Erica Gonzalez -
Jacqueline Dickey
Elisenda Costa -
Diana Cantu - Me
Jenny Park - Chris
Alexandra Gibson
Elizabeth Aljer -
Anita Gahir - Thor
Mary McTiernan -
Gina Larsen - Ft
Reiko Okada - Me
Brittany Nelson -

Girls 10-11

Alright, you get the point that in my younger years I played with and competed against some of the game's best. Am I trying to say that I am as good as them? Absolutely not. That would be ridiculous. Am I trying to say that I am so cool that I am friends with all these great players? No. I hardly knew them and they may or may not remember me—that is not the point. As I said this book is not about me trying to demonstrate how great I am.

I will now focus on tournaments where I performed well or won an award that reflected my playing ability. In 2001, I was the player of the year on the OJGF Tour and I won an award for the lowest stroke average. Here is a picture of me with that award.

In the summer of 2002, I played in the Future Masters and came in fifth place shooting 73-73. During the final round, I played with Harris English for the first time in my life and, holy shit, was he good! My dad had a "list" of golfers he thought were great. Believe me it was extremely tough to make this list. Of all the tournaments my father watched in the fifteen years of my golf career, only three golfers ever made the list. Harris was one of those players to make the list; it was during the final round of this tournament where he shot -4 that got him on my father's list. In my opinion, while Harris is a multiple PGA Tour winner, I think he should know that one of his greatest accomplishments is making my father's "list."

The following summer I played in the Future Master's once again but finished in last after making the cut. My mom was not pleased with my performance at this event and said, "Jason, if we are going to be spending all of this money on your golf, you need to start practicing." Before that tournament I really did not practice that much. I remember taking a golf lesson once a week and if I had a tournament that week I would practice a little more. So I want to thank my mom for giving me a kick in the ass and telling me to practice. Basically once I started high school I started practicing about six times a week. It's not like I became great just because I started to practice. However, I definitely noticed my game getting sharper. I actually call my twelve to fourteen years my "dark ages" because good tournaments were few and far between.

Onto my high school golf career. I went to high school at Miami-Palmetto Senior High. Although high school golf is not a big deal it was fun to play competitively but not really care. In golf, college scholarships are earned by playing in independent golf tours and achieving a high enough ranking. High school golf is very insignificant in the whole equation. That being said, I was either number one or two on my golf team. One of my teammates was actually a very good golfer who played Division I golf. I had a little bit of a rivalry with him to be top gun on the team. I was voted first team All-Dade three out of the four years, which essentially means that I was on the all-star team. On top of that I won three individual tournaments in high school.

I was not a superstar junior golfer, but I had some very respectable finishes. In the summer of 2005, I tied for seventh in the Future Collegiate World Tour (FCWT) National Championship. That same summer I had my best Future Masters Tournament, shooting 73-69-67 to tie for fifth place. In 2006, I placed in the top ten for the first time in an American Junior Golf Association (AJGA) event in Bedminster, New Jersey, at one of Donald Trump's golf courses. Trump made an appearance at the tournament and I have a signed flag from him. Who knew that I would have a president's autograph. My best junior golf tournament was an AJGA in Illinois in July 2007. I came in fourth place and shot rounds of 71-72-69. Who was the winner of the tournament? One Scott Langley, who absolutely decimated the field and would later become a member of the PGA Tour. That is the last junior tournament I will talk about.

I was not highly recruited out of high school when it came time for me to go to college. Growing up, I always wanted to go to the University of Florida (UF) to play golf. If I could not play for UF, I wanted to stay in Florida and play golf for one of the major Division I universities. As interested as I was in the Florida schools, they did not share the same interest in me. I could have stayed in Florida and maybe played Division II, but there was no way I was not playing Division I golf. I wanted to go to a major university, go to football games, and have as much of a college experience as possible, even though the life of a student athlete is very different from your average frat bro. Eventually, the University of

Colorado (CU) coach offered me an official visit to their campus. I liked what I saw and agreed to accept a small scholarship to attend. People are always surprised when I tell them I went to CU for undergrad. I suppose it is far for somebody from Miami to end up in the mountains. Knowing what I know now, the process of getting recruited is similar to college graduates seeking their first full time job. A lot of graduates are so fixated on their "dream job" that they do not take a more modest opportunity to further enhance their skills and get better at their trade. For example, a lot of individuals in finance want to work for the best banks, such as Goldman Sachs, right out of college even though that may be unrealistic. The University of Florida was my Goldman Sachs and where I really wanted to play, while the University of Colorado was my large bank that wasn't quite on the same level. However, UF did not want me and so I ended up playing for CU, where I learned my trade and my game improved dramatically.

My golf game really developed in college, although not at first, and not without growing pains. My first year, I played really badly and was uncomfortable with the team. It did not help that the older guys on the team were major assholes to me. I am friendlier with them now, even though the way they treated me was not the best. They did not do anything too bad, such as physical abuse or extreme hazing, but they were not good teammates in my eyes. They gave me a pretty damn hard time for anything I did. If I made the slightest error on or off the golf course they would rip me apart and I would not hear the end of it for weeks. It was unnecessary, but oh well. My freshman year was a real struggle: I ended up redshirting,[5] which was probably the best decision because even if I had qualified for a tournament I would have most likely performed poorly.

---

[5] Redshirting is when an athlete does not participate in competition for a year and gets to extend their eligibility.

I won the qualifier for the first event at the start of my redshirt freshman year and headed to my first college tournament in Albuquerque, New Mexico, to play in the Tucker Invitational. The University of New Mexico's golf course is a serious test of golf to say the least. I shot 235 for a stellar +19 and a solid ninetieth place finish. The rest of that fall season was equally as pathetic. I finished in eighty-first at Air Force's Golf Tournament, and finished eighty-sixth in UCLAs Tournament to wrap up the fall season. The spring season was basically going the same until San Diego State's Tournament in California. I hit an approach to about forty feet right of the pin. My coach was standing by the green and asked me, "Where were you trying to aim on that shot?" He was not mad at me but he wanted to know. I told him I was aiming for the center of the green. He said, "You should have been aiming at the pin on that shot." The honest truth was I had no idea why I should have aimed at the pin. After the round, the team did not play well and our coach was really ripping us apart. He called me out and said, "Jason, I never hear you ask any questions!" He was right—I needed to ask questions because I didn't know how to navigate a golf course properly in terms of where to hit my approach shots. I always played to the center of the green, which was a flawed strategy. Sure, there are times when you should play to the center of the green, but not all the time. After learning to leave my approaches below the hole, I felt that correct golf course management allowed me to be more aggressive. I started firing at more pins when the contours of the green and certain pin positions allowed for it.

This concept was not hard to learn, and it took me no time to figure out how to chart a green during practice rounds. I was never taught how to do it when I was younger and I was, unfortunately, too scared to ask questions earlier that season. I am very happy that my coach called me out on it as right after that tournament my scores started to improve dramatically. The last two tournaments of the season were Texas A&M's Event and the Big 12 Championship. I had respectable finishes in both tournaments, finishing in roughly thirtieth place in each event. The most important aspect from these two tournaments, however, was the fact that it was the first time in my life that I played golf correctly with good management and thought about where to leave my approach shots. My scores dropped, not because I was hitting better golf shots or making more putts, but because I was leaving my approach shots in the correct position.[6]

That summer I had two memorable tournaments: I shot 70(-2) in US Open local qualifying but unfortunately lost in a playoff to advance to sectionals; then in the US Amateur Qualifier, I shot 75-66(-1) but missed qualifying by two shots. That 66 was my lowest round at the time and one of my favorite rounds for reasons I will explain later.

My redshirt sophomore year was an improvement from my first year. While I did not do anything too spectacular that year, I had one good tournament in Bandon, Oregon. For those of you who do not know Bandon, Oregon is right on the Pacific Coast and we played the tournament in the middle of March when the weather is awful. I shot 76-71 during the thirty-six-hole day. The weather was calm throughout the first eighteen holes, but the wind really picked up over the second eighteen. I would say sustained winds of twenty miles per hour (mph) and gusts of over thirty mph. I played better in the tougher conditions for whatever reason. However, those conditions were tame compared to the final day.[7] When I say it was windy that day doesn't

---

[6] If you want to see a clip of me from the Big 12 Championship that year, you can watch the video on YouTube: https://www.youtube.com/watch?v=ssNgo_66724.

[7] The final round actually had a major delay because of the tsunami that devastated Japan in 2011. There was a chance the tremors from Japan would cause a tidal wave on the Oregon Coast, so we were possibly not going to play. It was eventually determined that the course wouldn't be hit by a tidal wave and we played.

do it justice. It was a hurricane out there! It was wet, it was cold, it was windy, and it was miserable. I must have had four layers of shirts and three layers of pants on. The wind was easily over twenty-five mph and certain holes on the coast were probably around forty mph. I remember hitting a wedge shot on a par-3 that was downwind and getting blown forward like Gary Player walking through one of his golf shots. I also remember hitting driver on a par-3 that was 170 yards long into the wind. I ended up shooting 74(+2) for the day. I believe I was one shot off the low round of the day. I finished in thirteenth place and it was the best finish of my college career at the time. That is one of the proudest rounds of my life.

My redshirt junior year was the first time I played in every single event; however, my only noteworthy accomplishment of that year was that I got my first top ten finish in CU's home tournament.

The summer between my junior and senior year I played some impressive golf. I will highlight two events. First, I shot my career low round in the Florida Amateur qualifier: a 63(-9) at Lago Mar Country Club—which I believe is still the course record today. In addition, I played in a mini tour event at PGA National on the Champ Course where the Honda Classic is held. I shot 71-68(-5); it would have been -1 for the pros because they play the course as a par 70, but they set it up differently.

My redshirt senior year was really a breakout year. Our season started off with a small tournament where only CU and Air Force Academy played in a fifteen-man stroke play event. I won that shooting 68-70(-4). The next week I won my first major tournament. The Gene Miranda Falcon Invitational. This was the same tournament that I finished in eighty-first three years earlier. I shot 68-71-68(-9). I was so proud. But not because I won the tournament—the most gratifying thing was how far I had come in my career at CU: from somebody who essentially had the shanks and struggled to break 80 my redshirt year to a Division I collegiate champion. I was so happy. To make things better my dad and brother flew out to that tournament. It was very special for me. I had a bad tournament after the Air Force event but bounced right back two days later and finished seventh in New Mexico's Tucker Invitational. This was the same course where I competed in my first collegiate event three years earlier and finished ninetieth. My best tournament of the spring was at the Bandon Dunes Championship where I finished in third place and tied with the number one amateur in the world at the time. My last good event was at the Wyoming Cowboy Classic where I finished in tenth place.

Unfortunately, my college career didn't end well. I played very poorly at my last two events: the Pac-12 Championship and NCAA Regionals. Despite playing like garbage at these last two events, they were at some of the best golf courses I have ever played in my life. The Pac-12 Championship was played at Los Angeles Country Club —one of the most exclusive golf courses in the world. Ronald Reagan was a member there and the Playboy Mansion borders the thirteenth or fourteenth tee box. Although completely bordered by hedges it was pretty cool to be that close to the Playboy Mansion. My college career finally came to a close at the NCAA Regionals which took place at the University of Arkansas golf course. This golf course is owned by Mr. Tyson. The chicken guy, not Mike. It is the hardest golf course I have ever played in my life. What stung the most about those last two tournaments was that if I had two solid tournaments, there was a good chance I would have been an All-American honorable mention. But I didn't get the job done and that's the way life goes. So after NCAA Regionals concluded, I became a professional golfer. Actually, as I hit my final putt I said to myself "pro."

After NCAA Regionals I had my college graduation and then it was time to get my professional career started. My first professional golf tournament was the Little Wind River Casino Saltwater Classic. Yes, that really was the name. I shot +7 for three days on a painfully easy golf course and earned a paycheck of $70. A few weeks later, I played in a Monday qualifier in Wichita, Kansas. I shot 71(-1) to miss a playoff by three strokes. I played pretty well on a tough golf course, but you know what playing pretty well in a Monday qualifier gets you? Absolutely nothing. The next event I played in was the San Juan Open in Farmington, New Mexico. I missed the cut shooting rounds of roughly 75 for three days. My only somewhat solid event that summer was a Dakotas Tour event in Vermillion, South Dakota. I shot rounds of 73-71-72(E) to come in twenty-third place. The rest of my summer in the Midwest was not very impressive either. I did one more Monday qualifier in Springfield, Missouri, where I shot 71(-1) and missed a playoff by five shots. It was not the greatest start to my professional career.

I moved back home to Miami and for the next year and a half or so I mostly did mini tour events in Florida. For the most part, I exclusively played on two mini tours—The Minor League Golf Tour in West Palm Beach and the West Florida Tour in the Sarasota area—and had one victory on each tour. I had a lot of solid finishes on both tours but won't highlight them since reading it would be tedious.

In regards to my Qualifying School (Q-School) efforts, my first attempt was in the fall of 2013. I breezed through prequalifying, shooting even for three days. Then in first stage, I shot even for four days and got knocked out at that stage. In January 2014, I did Q-School for the PGA Latinoamérica Tour and earned conditional status. Even though I had status on the tour, I didn't go down to South America that often. I flew down for two Monday qualifiers, but I didn't get into many tournaments because I had low priority conditional status. I did get into two tournaments in Argentina and Uruguay. Basically, the tournament director called me two days before the tournament and said, "Jason, you got into the tournament. Can you play?" He was essentially asking if I could fly half way around the world, plan a trip that costs $2,000, and if there was one delay, I was probably going to miss my tee time on Thursday. I declined to go both times because I was not given enough notice. I tried Q-School one more time in the fall of 2014. I got through first stage on the number, but played horrendously at second stage.

That, folks, essentially wraps up my golfing career.[8] Although I never made it to the Tour, I hope you can see that I gathered extensive experience across multiple levels of competitive golf. I have achieved my ten thousand hours at this game,[9] which I feel is important for me to show.

---

[8] If you want a clearer view of my playing results, go to jasonbgolf.com.
[9] Ten thousand hours is a reference to Malcolm Gladwell's book *Outliers*, in which he states that in order to achieve success or expertise in any field a person needs to dedicate approximately ten thousand hours toward that craft.

CHAPTER 3

My Mental Journey

As the saying goes, "Golf is ninety percent between the ears." Once you have the physical ability, I would say that is very true.

Around the age of twelve, I started to notice my anxiety on the golf course kick up a notch. If I had to guess, this was the beginning of the end for me. I'll never forget the first time my heart started to beat fast. I'm fairly certain I was twelve years old playing an event in Ponte Vedra Beach, Florida, at Pete Dye's Valley Course. I had a four-footer on the first hole for par when my heart started to beat rapidly and my arms started to shake. I remember saying to myself "this is different." Although I can't say with certainty, I believe I talked to my dad about this new feeling. This may have been the worst thing I could have done because I opened up a can of worms that would not close.

When I started playing golf at ten years old I did get nervous, but looking back it was a normal amount of nerves. For example, I would have butterflies at the beginning of a round, but was calm shortly after. A far cry from how excessive my nerves became as the years went on.

As a result of my golf anxiety increasing at age twelve, I saw my first sports psychologist. Let's call him Dr. BS. Since the golf tournament was in the city where he was located, my dad suggested that I see him. This was my first exposure to sports psychology. I believe I did a half-day session with him right before my golf tournament where he exposed me to the clichés of golf psychology such as "one shot a time," "stay in the present," "positive thinking," and other well-known sayings.

As time went on, it seemed that I developed different mental obstacles. For example, I noticed at thirteen that I developed a mental block when it came to score during a round. I would get significantly anxious whenever I was around -2. It didn't matter what part of the round it was. I think it was a form of self-sabotage, though I have no idea where it came from. It was like clockwork and extremely frustrating for me—almost as if I became mentally weaker for some mysterious reason. I didn't have that limitation at all when I first started playing golf. I remember when I was ten years old at the Optimist International, I was -5 through fourteen holes, which didn't faze me in the slightest. So I became very curious as to where this scoring barrier came from. This is why I became so obsessed with psychology. I knew I had issues that I needed to get over in order to be the best golfer I could be. Certain rounds I would hang around -2 and sometimes I would break through that number, going lower. But reflecting on it, I feel that I usually backed up to around even par most of the time when I had a good round going because of this bizarre anchor I had on myself. In sports psychology, this is referred to as a comfort zone.

Another struggle of mine was that I would become more anxious during the closing holes of a round. Once again, I didn't have this issue when I first started, but it became a real issue and drove me nuts. Despite working with mental coaches, knowing that every shot counts the same, doing my best to do "one shot at a time," and doing my pre-shot routine, I really struggled to rid myself of the shakiness I felt on the closing holes of most rounds I played in.

My father was with me throughout every single junior golf tournament I played in Florida (approximately 150). He was incredibly supportive. He drove me all around the state and provided me with the resources that go along with being a junior golfer. I am forever grateful for this. Having said that, I think he screwed up as well. After every round, my dad and I would discuss it. We would talk about what I could have done better, what were good shots, and what shots I needed to save, etc. All of that was fine, but there was also always a discussion about how I felt during the round. He would ask after every round, "How were you mentally?" At the time I didn't think it was a big deal. But thinking about it later in life, I think it was wrong of him to ask this after every round. To me it is comparable to constantly asking someone who is going through a tough time in life and asking how things are going, reminding them of the problem, instead of letting them get over the issue. Sure, it is nice that you are asking how they are feeling, but you are simultaneously reminding them that something is wrong and opening up a wound instead of letting them live life. That is how I felt when my dad would ask me how was I mentally—it was a constant reminder of my golf angst.

It became so ridiculous that we started to determine success on how I felt mentally and not on what I actually shot. It is hard to criticize my father because he was doing what he thought was best to help me; however, his methods were incorrect.

Because of these struggles, I was constantly seeking mental help. Or I should say, my dad was always seeking mental help for me. He would buy me books and audio tapes, and was always pushing me to see these "expert" sports psychologists. I would not want to go a lot of times, but my dad has a way of beating a dead horse until eventually I would succumb just so I wouldn't have to hear him anymore. I remember reading or hearing something about Gary Woodland saying a camera bothered him or something along those lines to his mom. His mom responded by saying, "Gary, if you are going to be a big-time athlete you need to deal with those things." Essentially, she was saying get over it. I wish my father had taken an approach like that. I would have been much better off if he said, "Jason, stop being the world's softest person and kick some ass." However, psychology is a thing in new millennium sports and the way to "get better" mentally.

Another struggle I had was I would become excessively nervous when people I knew or put importance on watched me. For example, I became nervous when college coaches followed me throughout my college recruitment process. Although I don't think that is unnatural, it still bothered me. It is very counterproductive and a slippery slope to get nervous in front of certain people. I remember one tournament I saw a gentleman, who was wearing a Duke University hat and shirt, following my group. As the tournament was in North Carolina, I thought it was the Duke University coach and became nervous as a result. When I found out later that it was just a regular person, I became infuriated with myself. I remember thinking I wasted all that mental energy and got nervous over nothing. All because I placed some "importance" on this college coach who was not even a coach but just a regular Joe Blow. I wish

I could say that I never got nervous in front of someone who I thought was important after that; unfortunately, it was something I continued to struggle with tremendously. I remember when I was eleven playing in the Doral Publix, I was quite nervous as my first golf coach watched me play a hole. At around the age of fifteen, I was, once again, fairly freaked out as my coach at the time watched me play a hole at the same junior golf tournament. I would even get nervous in front of family members. At a golf tournament in New Jersey, where my aunt, uncle, and grandma watched me play a couple of holes, you would have thought a gun was pointed at my head because my heart was racing so fast. When I was twenty, my cute girlfriend and her sister watched me play a few holes in West Palm Beach and I was again freaked out. My girlfriend was, at the time, the person I was most comfortable with, and yet I was terrified when she watched me that day. What I don't get is that my family and friends were there to support me—they wanted to see me play well—but I always perceived it as a threat when someone I knew watched me. If I didn't play well in front of them I was afraid they would say things like, "What the hell was that?" or "I thought you play this game every day."

Most sports psychologists would say that a golfer should only play golf for themselves and not play to impress others. While I do agree with that and tried not to focus on the people that were watching me, the fact is there was nothing I could do to get rid of my fear or nerves. It's not as if I always played badly when people I knew watched me, it just made the game a lot harder. This is what would occur: I would be playing golf feeling calm, but would become very shaky and nervous once I saw someone I knew. What's strange is that I never got nervous in front of my dad, his presence never fazed me—it was just other people I knew. I used to say I would have no issue playing in front of a million strangers, but playing in front of one person I knew was extremely daunting to me. Another peculiarity of this fear was that if a person I knew watched me from the beginning of the round it had less of an effect, but I hated it if they popped up somewhere during the round.

In addition to my nervousness, I had a very strong superstition. It began when I was twelve and dealt with eating food on the golf course. I was playing in a small tournament in Miami and was doing well during the final round. After I got a sandwich from the cart lady on the front nine, my playing competitor said to me, "You can't eat, you're playing well." I immediately knew it was the most absurd thing and responded, "That is the dumbest thing I have ever heard!" His comment didn't faze me that round, but moving forward I had an internal battle with myself when it came to food. For instance, if I was playing well, I was scared to eat any food even if I was starving and desperately needed energy. Food essentially became a momentum shifter: if I was playing well and ate, I would start to play badly, and it would have the opposite effect if I was playing badly. Despite many instances when I would eat while playing well and continued to play well, the superstition stuck with me. I will never understand why I took what this person said to heart. This guy was nowhere near the golfer I was; it's not like I looked up to this person or that it came from Tiger Woods' mouth—even that wouldn't have validated it.

When I entered college and started playing for the University of Colorado, my nerves intensified and I became more nervous about more things. The biggest mental block I had throughout college was playing in front of my head coach. In the five years that I was on the team, I only hit one golf shot in front of him where I was entirely calm. I suppose it's not abnormal to be uncomfortable playing in front of your head coach, but it makes college golf a lot harder. In fact, I have a friend who played college tennis and he told me he had the same struggles. I suppose it would be similar to someone who works an office job and has their boss looking over their shoulder checking their work—it's an uncomfortable feeling. I talked to some of my teammates about my feelings, but while most of them got over this anxiety pretty quickly, I never did. I tried to rationalize my feelings toward my coach by saying, "What is the difference between a golf shot whether he's watching or not?" or "Who cares what he thinks?" But nothing calmed me down. I'd shake so badly when he'd watch me hit shots in tournaments. I remember at a tournament in San Diego, I was butchering a hole and he was watching me the whole way. I think a soldier in war might have been calmer.

Besides my coach, there were certain teammates of mine that I felt more nerves toward than others. I entered the University of Colorado in a recruiting class of one of four freshmen and felt totally at ease with them. The teammates I struggled to stay calm in front of on the golf course were the upper classmen. This was probably because—as I mentioned earlier—they gave me a hard time my first year. So I was always afraid of hitting bad shots in front of them because they would rip me apart and give me an endless heap of crap if I did. For example, let's say I was playing a tournament and there was a backup on a par-3, if certain teammates were watching me I would be calm but if others were watching I would become pretty damn nervous. As a junior at a tournament in Hawaii, I was completely calm when two freshmen team-mates watched me play because, in a way, I felt superior to them. However, in other situations, such as when I would hit shots in front of a teammate who gave me crap, I would get pretty anxious.

I started to see a traditional psychologist when I was in Boulder to help with the excessive nerves I was battling. I would talk to this shrink about my golf rounds and the issues I talked about earlier in this chapter, such as getting nervous the last few holes, getting nervous in front of my coach, etc. And yet, the only thing I felt this guy accomplished was wasting my time and my parents' money. All we would do was rationalize situations, which never made me feel any better when a "stressful" situation would arise. For example, I played in the Dixie Amateur, an amateur tourna-ment in South Florida, one winter break. In the group behind me was Dan Marino's son. On one hole there was a backup and, as a result, Dan Marino was hanging around the tee box. I became anxious because I wanted to impress Dan Marino, though who knows if he even watched me hit the shot or not. I talked about this situation with the psychologist and we came to the following conclusion: let's say Dan Marino thinks I am terrible at golf, how does that affect me? Now let's reverse it and say Dan Marino thinks I am great at golf, how does that affect me? Since my life neither improves nor worsens in both instances, why should I care what he thinks?! This makes perfect sense logically and I tried to use that logic in similar situations, but it never worked. I struggled to calm down once I saw an anxiety trigger of mine. No rationalization, no deep breathing, or any mental "tricks" did anything for me. As a result, I don't believe in rationalization of fears as a solution because it never did anything for me.

In the summer after my sophomore year, I was pretty intrigued when my dad came across a mental coach who was not a psychologist. Rather he was an individual who was exceptional at his sport and competed at the highest level. Let's call him Mr. O. He marketed himself by saying that he wasn't a psychologist but had created a mental system that he used in high-pressure situations and allowed him to reach the pinnacle of his sport. I was intrigued by this because he was not a psychologist and actually gave a concrete mental system to reduce anxiety. Additionally, he was successful at his craft, unlike most golf psychologists who may not have been successful in their area of expertise, yet still give psychological advice on it. I was pretty over psychologists by that time and saw Mr. O as a breath of fresh air. His theory was that everyone has a "self-image" and a person can only perform as well as their self-image. For example, if you see yourself as someone who shoots 75 on a regular basis then that is what you will shoot for the most part. So let's say you shot -2 on the front nine, your self-image would get in the way and you would shoot +5 on the back nine. This sounded like it was hitting the nail on the head with one of my biggest issues of going very low. According to Mr. O, the way to improve or increase a person's self-image was by positive reinforcement. One technique to improve this area was to write out a mantra that you felt was the answer to the areas that needed improvement and place it in areas you go throughout your day. The language that was used in these mantras was of critical importance. The purpose was to help the individual become the type of person they desired to be, thus the mantra had to be written out as if the individual had already become that person. The mantra also was to be written out so that it describes what *needs* to be done to become that person. I will give examples of what my mantras were:

"I am totally focused on process when I play golf. I've taken a step toward becoming a top fifty collegiate golfer in the nation. I am more relaxed when I focus on process; I have a quieter mind when I focus on process. I am a consistent starter on the golf team, and I am helping my team by shooting better scores by focusing on process. I run a mental program for each shot. I am totally focused on process when I play golf."

Here is another mantra that I used:

"I am calm in front of my coach and teammates. I've taken a step toward becoming a top fifty collegiate golfer in the nation. I play better when I am calm; I am happier when I am calm. I run my system so that I remain calm in front of my coaches and teammates. I am calm in front of my coach and teammates."

Another key point of Mr. O's program was that a golfer needed to change their language to help increase their self-image. For example, an individual should never talk about the negative aspects of their round. If he or she must talk about things that went wrong, they have to use the word "needed." For example, let's say I played a round of golf where I drove the ball poorly and had four three-putts. According to Mr. O, you would never say, "I drove the ball terribly and putted like a clown with four three-putts." What you would say is, "I needed to drive the ball better and I needed to have four more two-putts." Essentially, he wanted golfers to direct their words and thoughts to what actually "needed" to be done instead of saying what went wrong. By using this language, one's self-image should increase and the individual should perform better in the future. One thing I will say on this matter is that it is painfully annoying to hear golfers talk about their bad rounds in detail. On the flip side if a golfer spoke negatively such as saying, "I suck at golf," they will decrease their self-image and get worse at golf. He even said that if you hear other people talk about their bad golf shots it will adversely affect you so you need to stay away from people who speak negatively. In addition, seeing bad golf shots was detrimental to one's self-image. So if you saw someone shank a shot or miss a putt it was not good for your self-image. I internalized this information entirely too much and should have seen the flaws in his theories. I remember I was playing a round during a mini tour event and my playing partner was telling me how the person he played with the day before made a triple bogey on the same hole we were on. I never asked the player to tell me about this, he just started talking about it out of the blue. I became nervous because I had heard something negative and bad imagery had been presented. I thought I was going to play the hole poorly, and ultimately didn't play the hole as well as I should have.

An additional part of the agenda consisted of maintaining a mental journal, detailing everyday golf activities, whether that was a round of golf, a practice session, etc. In the journal, a golfer would write about what they did well that day, what needed to improve, and the percentage of times they executed their routine. The purpose of the percentage was that Mr. O judged success on how many times the routine was performed successfully and not on what a golfer shot. According to him and many others, being results oriented causes anxiety. That is why the main objective should be to count the percentage of times a routine was successfully performed, not score.

Lastly, Mr. O had a theory on how to gain mental control. He, like other sports psychologists, said you must become immersed in your pre-shot routine. According to him, if a golfer is engaged in their pre-shot routine, it's impossible to focus on anything else because the conscious mind can only focus on one thing at a time—and it's therefore impossible to have intrusive or negative thoughts. The majority of our sessions were spent on creating a pre-shot routine. We tried to get it so ingrained that he would use a timer to see how well I could execute and repeat it. There was also a post-shot routine. The purpose of this was to increase the self-image. No matter what kind of golf shot was hit—good, mediocre, or pathetic—you always performed your post-shot routine. This entailed doing the correction of the golf shot that would have made it optimal. So let's say you blocked a putt, you would perform the post-shot routine by doing a putting stroke where you struck the putt with a square face or the correction of the physical task. If you hit a perfect shot, you would repeat the movement. According to him, no matter what kind of shot was hit, your self-image would improve by imprinting the correction. Later in the book I will describe my criticism with this mental system.

Before I get into pro golf and my mental journey during that stage of my life, I would like to share a few journal entries from my mental journal. My first entry was on July 8, 2012. I actually had a journal starting three years before that, but I think I threw it out in pure disgust one day. I wish I hadn't because there was probably a ton of great material in there. These entries should give you a pretty good idea of my struggles.

July 8, 2012

"Played the front nine with Jessica and starting was pretty nervous. After a few holes was normal. Don't know why I even started off nervous. We weren't playing for anything. Then I saw my assistant golf coach on the range and hit a few shots in front of him and got anxious. I used to not get nervous in front of him, now I do."

July 12, 2012

"Did a tournament for the school, something totally for fun, and was nervous on the range. Got more nervous when seeing my assistant coach again. I remember the athletic director played in front of me and I thought to myself, 'I bet I would have been pretty nervous playing with him.' It's almost as if I am getting anxiety thinking about getting anxiety. I had a bad round, not because of anxiety, I just struggled and at the end of the round my assistant coach asked what happened. How was it possible I shot 75? I didn't really care about the round, but I felt a charge rush through me. I have to figure out how to make golf fun again."

July 15, 2012

"I think I realized that what makes me nervous is having the coaches talk to me or criticize me. If that's what I'm nervous about then there's really absolutely nothing to worry about. They can't do anything to you. Nobody can. You can simply nod your head and go on with your life if you disagree with what they say. It's time to toughen up."

Not all of my entries were miserable tales about my nerves and anxiety. There were moments of hope and triumph. This next journal entry is about the time I played with Jonathon Kaye—one of the most influential rounds of my life. What made it more powerful was that I didn't know who I was playing with. While playing, he was telling me about his golf accomplishments (not in a braggadocios way, I had asked him)—such as winning the Colorado Open, getting through Q-School, playing on Tour, and winning a couple of times—but I never connected the dots as to who he was. It wasn't until after the round when somebody asked "What's up JK?" that I realized I had just played with Jonathon Kaye. It was better that I didn't know who I played with because had I known I would have been nervous. Here is my journal entry from that day:

July 16, 2012

"Today I played with Jonathon Kaye and his wife Jennifer. I didn't know who I was playing with until the end of the day. I didn't know I was playing with a PGA Tour winner. It was so interesting to play with him because I was intrigued with his personality and the type of person he was, not with his golf game. It was better I had no clue who he was. He was singing the whole round and teasing his wife. It looked like he was just chilling on the golf course. Some of his stories were very interesting since I got to know what kind of person he was. He was kicked off of his golf team, he chewed out somebody in the US Open because they weren't raking the bunkers—basically, he totally did what he wanted and I just know he did not care about what anybody thought. This is how I know I want to be. He played golf like I play basketball talking shit and having fun. A story I loved was when he walked off the thirteenth hole in a qualifier because the twenty hours[10] were up. That just shows how he truly only cared about himself and not his

---

[10] The NCAA has a rule that athletes across all sports are not allowed to spend more than twenty hours per week practicing or competing while in season.

coaches. I would never do anything like that, but it's the mindset I want. Basically he was not soft and I think that is what my problem is, my true root cause. I just need to toughen up and have fun. I think this may have been one of the most important rounds of my life, a major light bulb has gone off. I asked him if he was able to stay calm on Tour and he said he just never gave a shit and I totally believe him."

I lost a lot of my anxieties after playing with Jonathon. My competiveness was through the roof and I played some of the best golf of my life that summer. I shot the low round of my life. I came in twenty-ninth in the Colorado Open, which is a pretty solid finish. I shot 71-68 at the course where they hold the Honda Classic in a mini tour event. So I had a lot of success that summer. I really attribute a lot of it to that round with Jonathon. I just had it mentally. I wanted to destroy everyone every time I teed it up. I was ecstatic and excited that I lost my fears. But not so fast—the nerves kicked back in once I started my last year of college golf. I got off to a very hot start my fifth year in college, winning the first two events, but even though I had won I knew I wasn't as mentally calm or hard as I was after playing with Jonathon.

In the spring semester of 2013, I started to see a traditional psychologist to try and help me with my golf issues. Let's call her Dr. L. She was actually very good and helped me out. She definitely helped mitigate my golf anxiety, even if I didn't completely get rid of it. Her main thing for me was to be very accepting of my thoughts and not beat myself up for having them. That it was okay to feel nervous no matter how irrational. I had always criticized myself for having certain thoughts because the golf psychologists I saw had me believe that I should never have intrusive or negative thoughts. Dr. L had a totally different perspective. She said, "You don't have control over thoughts, just accept what comes along and don't give them so much power." For example, a person may think if they see a plane, "I hope that plane doesn't crash." Basically, she was saying humans have intrusive thoughts and there is nothing wrong with having them.

After graduating college, I can't tell you how excited I was to turn professional and not deal with my college coach, workouts, thirty-six-hole days, or other things that bothered me about college golf. I figured all of my mental issues would disappear and I was going to make a boatload of money.

My very first professional golf tournament was the Little Wind River Casino Saltwater Classic in Riverton, Wyoming. I was so excited for my first pro tournament where I could make $$$. But I didn't get over my issues. I remember a wave of anxiety rushing over me when I saw a college teammate, someone who gave me a lot of crap, at the tournament. I was excessively nervous on the shot I hit in front of him. My coach was clearly not the issue—my phobia of being judged had nothing to do with him. I was the issue.

My debut summer of pro golf was not good. I stayed out in the Midwest and traveled a decent amount with some of my former teammates who were older than me. I remember at these tournaments I felt so judged by them. I would get nervous and anxious in front of them. I would check tee times for the day in hopes that I would not be paired with them or be in the group directly behind or in front of them. That way they could not see my shots. For example, I was paired with one of my former teammates in the Wyoming Open. I was so nervous going into this round because I felt I was going to be judged. I remember driving to the round blasting heavy metal and yelling at the top of my lungs in an attempt to psych myself up. I wanted to get the nerves out of me and replace them with anger. It did not work. I was so uncomfortable the whole round and shot +6 on an excruciatingly easy golf course. I was calm when I was paired with him again the next day. For some reason, after playing with somebody once, I would calm down the following day if the individual was somebody I got anxious in front of. This is such a bad mentality because pro golfers don't have time for such garbage. They can't afford to feel uncomfortable in front of somebody for a whole round and then feel okay the next day—there's no room for that type of nonsense. It is unacceptable and they will lose money. Pros need to be rock hard from the get-go to make it in golf. I'm not even sure being rock hard is necessary, they just can't be fazed by anxieties like that.

The following is a journal entry that describes my frustration with my mental battles:

August 5, 2013

"I have had a tough start to pro golf. I remember how excited I was to do this, and I still am, but I need to figure out my mind. I am so tired of being nervous around people I know. It's so ridiculous. I somewhat understood getting nervous around coach but I don't understand why I get nervous around people I know. I have had this forever. There was a person I thought was my roommate and I became nervous. When I realized it wasn't him, I calmed down. I didn't care when he watched at NCAA Regionals in Arkansas. I think I have conditioned myself to get nervous around people I know."[11]

That September I signed up to Q-School for the first time. It was the first year Q-School had been reorganized for the Web.com instead of the PGA Tour. I breezed through prequalifying, which put me through to first stage at a golf course called Grasslands Country Club in Lakeland, Florida. I remember checking the results from the year before to see what got through the qualifier: it was -12. I remember saying to myself, "Holy shit, I have never gone that low before." But something beautiful happened. I said to myself, "I don't have a second to waste on my anxiety or else I'm not going to get through." It was the best I have ever been mentally at a golf tournament. I was so angry and focused on the fact that I had to play well or else I wouldn't get through. I remember my very first approach I hit the pin and proceeded to birdie the first two holes. I was so laser-focused right from the get-go. I will highlight my journal entry from the last day. Even though I talk about some nerves, my mind was great that week.

October 11, 2013
- Was the best mentally this day of all the days.
- Figured I had to shoot -4 to have a chance.
- Shot even on the front then -3 on the back.
- Felt like I needed to make every shot. Had a good mindset, sense of urgency.

[11] My college roommate is someone I am very comfortable with so getting nervous in front of him didn't make sense. What was even more peculiar was that at NCAA Regionals, my last college tournament, he watched me play and I didn't care. I don't know what the difference was. What I meant by conditioning myself was that I felt like I was one of Pavlov's dogs where I had trained myself to become nervous if I saw somebody I knew on the golf course.

- On eighteenth hole had a ten-footer for birdie and became anxious.
- I actually needed to shoot -6 to qualify, not -4.
- So my issue with this mindset of picking a number to score is that I don't really know how well to do a lot of the time. Or let's say I am leading a golf tournament and it is the other way where I am being chased.
- Basically, I need to figure out how to have the feeling of I must make this (shot). No matter the situation, what round it is, what hole it is, because I can't fake the feeling, although I was able to get it more this week.

As good as I was mentally, I still did not advance. I shot even par for four days, and, unfortunately, it was not like this tournament was a breakthrough for me mentally. I was never really able to replicate that mindset again.

Around November 2013, I was very upset about a situation that revolved around my ex-girlfriend. Let's call her "Queen G." She started dating "M," the brother of one of my closest friends, who I was close with as well. It was something I did not take well, to say the least.

I started dating my ex-girlfriend when I was sixteen years old. I met her in a history class we had together and we went to prom together. I remember my first impression was not being able to decide whether this girl was super sexy or super cute. We started hanging out a lot. Her friends and my friends became friends and we became a crew. I would say that we dated consistently for about six months before we broke up for the first time. But we were on and off throughout college. Though we did go through stretches of not talking to each other for extended periods, there was nobody who knew me better, who knew my secrets like she did. I don't know about anymore, but for a long time it just seemed like no matter how much time passed with us not talking we were able to pick up right where we left off. We were very comfortable with each other for so many years.

We were both single after I moved back home in September 2013. I had a decision to make of whether or not to pursue her and try to date her again. I ultimately chose to pursue other girls because I felt I needed to experience other girls at the time. She was the only girl I had really dated so I figured I needed to explore other options to make sure I really liked her. I was also afraid that if I started to date her at age twenty-three that would be it. I was going to get married and I wasn't ready for it. In reality, I have nobody to blame but myself for not pursuing her. Although there was technically nothing wrong with M dating her, I didn't take it well. I even talked about it with my parents and my dad said, "You had the chance to pursue her and you didn't. You made a decision to pursue other girls. It's like you are Monday morning quarterback. You decided to pursue other girls so you know what you should do? Pursue other girls!" He was correct logically, but I couldn't take it emotionally. It upset me so much. I felt totally betrayed by both of them. I remember when Queen G called me to tell me they were dating, we hadn't spoken for months and after some small talk she said, "I have to tell you something and it's going to hurt you." Before she said another word I knew exactly what it was, I had suspected they were together for a while. I don't remember exactly what I said but the censored version was something along the lines of, "Screw you, I knew it, I knew it, don't call me again!"

As time went on and I matured, I realized that I was in the wrong to be upset about the situation. It was not my right to deny either of them the right to be with each other. But at the time it definitely affected me negatively.

The situation also affected my golf game at times; it was my Achilles heel. If it entered my mind I would become so depressed and just lose motivation. I feel for most people this would have been a very motivating situation. They would want to show their ex-girlfriend that they made a mistake, but it didn't work that way for me. There were times in golf tournaments where I would think of my ex with M and I just wanted to cry. It messed so much with my golf game. Here is one entry that describes what I went through during US Open Local Qualifying:

May 7, 2014

- Dreamt about the Queen G and M situation. Not exactly sure what my dream was about. Maybe about seeing them for first time and how I would react.
- In tournament, started to think about the two of them. More about M. It gave me such a timid, quivering feeling.
- Thought about it for the first few holes, forgot about it, then it came back. I did everything in my power to distract myself. Spelt words backwards, got angry.
- There was a point in my round when I was getting angry on purpose and I nearly lost it. Then just felt like crying because I was so frustrated and helpless with my mind.
- Toward the end of the round when I felt helpless, I started to ask myself, what do I need to do to stop my mind? Do I need to start smoking weed? Do I need to become religious?

- I tried the religious/spiritual route the last few holes. On a putt on my third to last hole I just said, "God let me stop thinking about this and let me make this putt."
- I started to think, do I need to start going to Temple? Then I started to think if people put their faith in something that has no proof of existing or knowing it's there, such as God, then why can't I?
- The last few holes I started to pray to the "Golfing God" and I put my faith in it.
- I felt I enjoyed this because it took the control out of my hands. I am susceptible to too many phobias and irrationalities that I have somewhat lost faith in myself.
- If I put my confidence in something outside of myself maybe I will do better.
- I realize this is kind of absurd but I feel my thoughts and feelings are absurd, yet they are very real to me. So, why can't I put my faith in something that is equally absurd but real to me?
- My college coach used to say do whatever it takes to believe in yourself. So that is somewhat what I am doing, just in a different form.
- What do I have to lose at this point?

As described, I started to try another mental approach with the Golfing God. But as I continued to play golf I was having the same issues over and over and my frustration was growing more and more. I really started to try absolutely everything. I pretended to be an actor of sorts and put myself in the mindset of golfers that I felt had great confidence. I describe this process in the next entry:

February 6, 2014

"I am going to do something different tomorrow. I am going to pretend I am Jordan Spieth and I am going to feel how he would feel on shots—which is just knowing they are going to be good. When I am doing well I am going to want more. I was thinking in my head how if I was an amateur how confident I would be. When people would show up I would say, 'Good, now I can give them a show.' I could feel my body language change. I would not settle for a score because all I would want to do is set a course record. Every hole would be such an opportunity. I am really excited to do this tomorrow and probably forever. There is no reason I can't feel this way as a pro."

My next few journal entries show more of the same issues and continued frustration.

February 8, 2014

"Did the Jordan Spieth mentality today, overall felt pretty good. Still noticed a little bit more anxiety toward the end, but it was better. Still not good enough. I am feeling very discouraged. I am starting to think my mind is unconquerable. A very big deciding factor is Puerto Rico. If I feel anxious around my old teammates I'll know that I'm not going to get over my mental issues. I don't want to quit. I must stay present-minded, calm around them, and want to show off. But I have decided that this is the deciding event."

What I meant in this entry was that I and many of my college teammates were participating in the Monday qualifier in Puerto

Rico for the Tour event there, so if I got nervous in front of them—whether it was on the practice green, range, anywhere—I knew I was up shit creek with my mind.

For the Puerto Rico Open there are kind of two chances to qualify for the tournament: there is the local qualifier which occurs on the Friday before the tournament and the regular Monday qualifier. The winner of the local qualifier gets a spot in the tournament. I was paired with one of my college teammates in the local qualifier. I stayed with a different college teammate of mine at this event and he asked me if I had ever played with one of our teammates in a tournament. I kind of spazzed out on him, saying, "Does it really matter who I play with? I don't care who I play with, it doesn't matter who I am paired with." He did not mean anything by it, he was just asking a simple question, but I took it personally because of my issues. Well, the round did not go well. I was excessively nervous as a result of being paired with my college teammate and upset with myself for being nervous. I was totally fine in the Monday qualifier since I was paired with a random person. I played fairly well, shooting -1, even though that missed a playoff by five shots.

I was so upset that I was still getting nervous in front of my teammates that I had to try something different: I called one of my older teammates who I became the most anxious in front of and talked to him. I told him my issues and if he had any advice for me. It didn't really matter what advice he gave me, I was doing it for myself. I thought maybe admitting my vulnerability to him would help me to get rid of my symptoms. So I told him that I get nervous in front of people I know and asked if he had any advice for me. He told me that I was not focusing on my pre-shot routine enough, which was standard mumbo jumbo in my book, but then he said something pretty interesting, "It is not like the golf ball knows who is watching or what is going on." I interpreted that as the golf ball is unbiased and unemotional. I really liked it. I tried to think of myself as a golf ball, an emotionless entity.

In April 2014, I started to do some research on meditation and I came across Transcendental Meditation (TM). This is probably the most famous of all meditation techniques because of celebrity endorsement. This is the meditation that was popularized when Maharishi Mahesh Yogi taught the Beatles how to meditate, and it has since been heavily marketed by celebrities. I couldn't care less about what celebrities do, except there were also testimonials of people who overcame their various issues with the help of TM. I remember hearing about a soldier who got over his post-traumatic stress disorder with TM, which made me think, "If a soldier can get over legitimate issues like that, then there is a chance my irrational fantasies could also go away." The way that TM works is that you meditate twice a day for twenty minutes. You are given a mantra and you repeat it over and over and over, but it's okay for the mind to drift away from the mantra. It's explained that when your mind drifts from the mantra you are breaking down stress. The instructors also state that people have breakthroughs at different times—some have it immediately and others have it after months or years. I did TM pretty consistently for about six months and it didn't do much for me.

Because of all my mental issues, I wasn't making money on the golf course and started to worry about my future. My parents and I came up with a plan in order for me to play my best. Throughout the years I noticed that I played my best when I had the feeling of my back being against the wall. For example, I would start to play incredibly when I was a little bit behind the cut line because I felt I had to. In addition, a very big fear I had when I was playing was that if golf didn't work out my future would be in jeopardy. I had never worked before as I was always playing golf and traveling. I had no work experience and really felt like I was going to be in a hole if I didn't make it with golf. So we decided to come up with a contract that would force me to achieve positive results in tournaments and if I didn't I would be forced to move on with life. I was also hoping the contract would create a sense of urgency. It was essentially a sales quota and if I didn't meet it, I would be fired. Here is a copy of the contract.

April 20, 2014

We, David Burstyn and Clara Milikowski, will continue financial support of Jason Burstyn's professional golf career only if these performance criteria are met by August 31, 2014:

Seventy-five percent of cuts made

One top 3 finish

Two top 5s

Three top 15s

Three top 25s

- Minor League one day events count as half a tournament toward criteria
- Excludes top twenty
- Web.com Qualifier only counts toward criteria for top three and five

- US Open Local Qualifier counts as half a tournament toward criteria
- Only toward top three

If these criteria are not met the only way to continue funding is a win in a multiple day event, getting through a Monday Web.com and making cut at it, or making $30,000 in prize money.

David Burstyn

Clara Milikowski

Jason Burstyn

I did not think about the contract much after signing it. I ended up fulfilling those obligations. I moved to Tampa that summer and played in the West Florida Golf Tour. I played fairly well, breaking even in terms of money for the most part. But I still didn't feel I was over my issues.

After the summer in Tampa, I moved back to Miami and recall looking at various mini tour scores. I looked at the results from the Hopkins Tour—which I was familiar with after playing in an event that summer. The tour did not play difficult courses but the scores were still unbelievably impressive, with players scoring extremely low. I recall looking at one event and seeing that Smylie Kaufman won with something around -20 for three days. I told my parents, "I am starting to lose the faith. I see these scores that people are shooting and I am just not doing it. I think it's time to move on." My reasoning was the entry deadline for Web.com Q-School was coming up and I had to decide whether or not it was worth more than $5K to play in Q-School. My parents convinced me that I should do it. I had put this many years into golf and it would be ridiculous to not do Q-School. They said forget the contract since they weren't keeping tabs on it and do Q-School. I agreed. It would've been stupid not to do Q-School after all the years of effort.

I didn't have to go through prequalifying that year because I had Latin America status. That meant I started at first stage and advanced. Second stage was in Panama City, Florida, at the Bad/Ugly Golf Course. I remember my dad asked if I wanted him to go to Q-School. Honestly, I didn't because I wanted to be as calm as possible and had started to develop some nerves toward him on the golf course. I also had a friend caddie for the week, though I didn't really want a caddie either because I knew I would be calmer on my own, but I also didn't want to carry my bag. I remember telling myself, "If you get nervous because of your father and caddie then you're not meant to make it, so say yes to both." I was so nervous starting the tournament all because of my dad and caddie watching. It had absolutely nothing to do with the fact that it was second stage. I promise that was not it. If I had been on my own I would have felt much better, but you cannot live your life in a box.

Here is my last journal entry which came from second stage, when I was at rock bottom with my golf career:

November 19, 2014

"I have never felt so miserable at a golf tournament. I have come to resent my biggest supporter, my dad. I have never played a round of golf where I had no fight in me. I just want to curl up and cry. After the round he didn't get mad at me and said very loving words but it didn't matter. There was nothing he could say that would have been right. I am just so tired of it. I feel like a twenty-five-year-old infant. Nothing has changed in fifteen years. 'You want a sandwich? What happened there? How were you mentally?'[12] I wonder how I became this way: talented, yet so plagued by my mind. It's only the second day of the tournament and I want it to end so badly. Not because I am playing bad, I just hate how I feel. I hate how I feel toward my dad. How is anyone supposed to have a life like this? I am in the hotel and feel so defeated. My mind has made me afraid and nervous of things that aren't real. What really pisses me off is that once I stop playing golf I am pretty sure I will lose all this shit. I want to become independent. I wish I could fund myself as a golfer, but then it's like what is so good about this life or job? Even now when I am so out of the tourney I feel like I can't let go of my anxieties and let them rest because of people's judgments. I have become afraid to say or do things because I believe it will come back to haunt me. It's so much garbage. I feel like golf has handcuffed me. But it's all me and no one else's fault—I didn't march to the beat of my drum. I just feel like fuck is the perfect description—just **FUCK**! This time it feels different though: this is complete disgust, defeat, and exhaustion. I

---

[12] What I meant by "You want a sandwich?" and all those other quotes is that these are things my father would ask at golf tournaments throughout the years.

have been frustrated about golf plenty of times before but nothing like this. I have two more days and in the past I know my mentality would be 'let's do something legendary.' Currently I feel like here comes more torture."

I had had it with golf and my mind. I knew it was the end of the road when I had no fight left in me to try to turn my rounds around. If someone is at second stage and they have no fight, something is wrong. Especially for me. I am one of the biggest grinders when it comes to golf, I was so good at bouncing back after bogeys and bad situations. But after fifteen years at the game my gas tank was officially empty—I was DONE.

CHAPTER 4

My Criticism of Golf/Psychology/ Commentators/"Experts"

GOLF CULTURE

Having spent the majority of my life around the sport of golf it's safe to say that it is what I am most passionate about. When somebody is immersed in an activity or industry over a long period of time they are more adept at being able to notice the positives and negatives within their area of expertise. Since the majority of my story is critical of golf, I will focus on topics that surround the game and what I believe are flaws within it.

For example, there is an expectation that golfers should act in a very particular way or else it's considered bad etiquette. Golf commentators really perpetuate this image. They love the guys who smile constantly and try to make them the game's poster children. An example of this is Phil Mickelson; all you ever hear about this guy is how he is constantly smiling, how nice of a guy he is, how he treats the fans so well, and blah blah blah blah. If they want to talk about how good of a golfer he is that is fine. I just can't stand it when the media and commentators try to create a Mr. Nice Guy or role model image of certain golfers. They have no idea what a person is like or what they do in their personal lives. I'm sure there are plenty of prominent golfers who are complete scumbags and live scandalous lives. The point I am trying to make is that PGA Tour golfers aren't necessarily angels, although this is the image that the PGA Tour tries so hard to create. The audience is not tuning in because golfers may or may not be good individuals. I personally couldn't care less what a person does with their money or life. I don't care if a PGA Tour golfer is the biggest jerk or the most charitable person on the planet. As far as I'm concerned, the only attribute a golfer should be praised for is his/her incredible golfing ability, other than that, the media and commentators should stop portraying them as great human beings.

One of my favorite people in the world is Charles Barkley because he says what's on his mind and doesn't try to please everyone. One of my favorite lines of his is, "Just because I dunk a basketball doesn't mean I should raise your kids." What he was referring to was being a role model and trying to act in a certain way that perpetuates a squeaky clean image. I agree with him that an athlete shouldn't have to act in a certain way so that the public will like or see them as a role model.

Another observation of mine that plays into this image of golfers is that they are not supposed to get angry or show emotion. When a golfer does get angry, they're usually ridiculed by commentators. For example, I have seen Jon Rahm get pissed in tournaments and, when he does, commentators often say something along these lines, "That is his only weakness," or "He needs to get that under control." I will never understand why becoming visibly upset is seen as a character flaw. And who is to say that Rahm isn't under control? He has clearly proven he is in control. Quite often when I watch football and a team is performing poorly the camera will show a player on the team yelling at his teammates in an effort to promote some sort of positive change. Since showing outward emotion is part of the norm in football, there is no issue. You would probably hear something along the lines of, "Wow, he is a really fiery competitor!"

Rocco Mediate said it well in an interview with Feherty; he said that pro golfers are killers. I like to say that PGA Tour golfers are "killers in collared shirts." But all that's perpetuated is the Mr. Nice Guy image of what a golfer should be and that's not the way it is. I feel that I became a Mr. Nice Guy because I bought into this image of how a golfer should act and it definitely hurt me. I was too soft to make it. I needed more killer in me. I read an article from Golf.com where Rocco discusses the playoff against Tiger Woods in the 2008 US Open. In the article, he describes how everyone in the world wrote him off in the playoff, but he felt he was better than Tiger and knew he was going to win. I wish more stories like this were highlighted instead of tales of golfers being nice, humble, or "doing things the right way"—they should show more of a killer instinct.

Along the lines of proper behavior, golfers shouldn't curse because it's not proper etiquette. The amount that golfers curse is probably the same as other athletes but it is seen as unacceptable for golfers because it's a "gentlemen's game." There are so many instances in golf tournaments where viewers will hear players curse. For example, I was watching the 2015 Frys.com Open and the camera was on Brendan Steele. He made a bogey on the fourteenth hole on the final day and the camera caught him saying, "This fucking hole." I loved it and who cares that he said it. But some people may say "He should be a good role model for kids and shouldn't say things like that." Golfers are not angels, nor should we be expected to be. Go on YouTube and type in "pro golfers cursing" and there will be hundreds of examples. It's not a big deal—who cares? The fact that golf has this quasi pretentious image really bothers me.

Humility is another value that golfers are supposed to exude. They are not allowed to be cocky or show extreme confidence or else the media will try to knock them down. The best example of this is Patrick Reed after he won the WGC at Doral, he said "I am one of the top five players in the world." The amount of heat that he got for it was absolutely ridiculous. First, he wasn't that far off. Based on the numbers he was probably ranked around twentieth in the world at the time. I loved that he said that. You don't really hear golfers talk like that as they're expected to be humble. Imagine if it was another sport. For example, it seems that it is the norm for boxers to show extreme confidence whether that be Muhammed Ali proclaiming "I am the greatest" or Floyd Mayweather saying one of his many lines of braggadocio. The cultures of these two sports are different: in boxing it's seen as having belief in yourself, but it's seen as being arrogant in golf. You know which sport has it right and which has it wrong? I think you know my answer to that. Patrick Reed is one of my golfing heroes because he exudes confidence and swagger and I applaud him for saying what he said. I love athletes who challenge the status quo. Why people in the golfing world label outward confidence or cockiness as a bad trait is beyond me.

GOLF COMMENTATORS

My next set of issues lies with golf analysts and the topics they frequently discuss. They talk about certain theories that are completely fictitious or have no way of being proven, yet present them to their audiences as fact.

For example, in regards to experience, commentators are always saying how the more experienced player on Tour has an advantage over a less experienced one. They will assert, if a rookie on Tour is in contention, that he will struggle because he is inexperienced. They also discuss how pro golfers need to "learn to win," but need to fail a few times before they can "learn to win." There are so many counterexamples to this common school of thought. Let me ask the golf talking heads this: How in the world did Russel Henley win his first PGA Tour event his rookie year? How did Emiliano Grillo do the same thing in the Frys.com Championship? How did Ben Curtis win the British Open in the first major he ever played? How did Sebastian Cappelen win his first Web.com Tour event after Monday qualifying into that event? How did Ben Kohles win the first two Web.com Tour events he played in? How did Jordan Spieth dominate everyone so quickly?

The simple answer to these questions is that experience is overrated. Yet, you'd think that nothing else matters with the constant discussion from golf analysts. According to their logic, every Tour rookie should miss each cut and every veteran should be at the top of the leaderboard. The simple fact is that all of these players know how to play golf. They have been playing since they were little kids and being "inexperienced" as a pro isn't a real thing. Commentators need to stop talking about experience like it's an advantage.

Onto my biggest pet peeve: golf commentators' discussion of nerves—every bad shot has to do with nerves. The worst thing that these people perpetuate into golf culture is this constant conversation about "nerves." Whenever you watch a golf tournament on Sunday, the amount of times the word nerves, or some variation of it, is spoken is a bit much. Especially since they have no way of knowing what a player is thinking or feeling. What's interesting to me, however, is that nerves aren't really talked about on the first two days of a golf tournament—I suppose commentators got together and decided that nerves don't exist on Thursday or Friday. If a golfer is toward the top of the leaderboard on Friday, commentators will often say something to the extent of, "But will he be able to handle the nerves on the weekend?" This is completely ridiculous, by pure simple logic. You can argue that the first two rounds are the most important because if a golfer plays badly the first two rounds, they will not make the cut or any money. But these commentators are obsessed with Sunday—and all of its "holiness"—for some reason, and place more weight on the last day. This is something that irks me and it makes me cringe when I hear any discussion about nerves on Sunday. There is a line that most people who watch the Masters know. Every year when the final group makes the turn, you can bet that somebody will say something along these lines, "And it doesn't begin until the back nine on Sunday at Augusta." Really?! I have never heard more absurd words in my life. Here's a news flash: a shot on the third hole is worth as much as the fourteenth, as the thirty-second, as the fifty-third as the sixty-first, and as the seventy-second. I am hopeful every year when a commentator says that line that someone will correct them or make fun of them, saying something like, "Actually, the tournament started on Thursday; Friday and Saturday are just as important as the back nine on Sunday." According to this cliché line, everyone who missed the cut is okay because, "Hey, it doesn't start till the back nine on Sunday." Obviously, I know it's just a saying—and who knows if commentators even believe it or just want to say a catchy phrase—but it exemplifies so much of what is wrong with golf commentators. When I was in second stage of Q-School, after sixty-three holes and nearly in last, I turned to my caddie and said, "Second stage doesn't start till the back nine on the Bad/Ugly Course" just to make fun of the saying. People need to stop saying that immediately.

In fact, this school of thought occurs in other sports. In basketball, for example, players who make free throws toward the end of the game are considered "clutch." Well, last time I checked a free throw made in the beginning of the game counted the same as the end. Everyone in sports is obsessed with how the end of a game/tournament goes, which is not logical to me. But I will stick to golf since that's my area of expertise.

My college coach had a flawed rule that demonstrates my point of why it's wrong to put extra importance on final holes/ rounds. The rule was: on the last three holes of a qualifier or any non-tournament round, if any member of the golf team was over par for the last three holes, they had to wake up in the morning and do a light cardio session. It was nothing too bad, just annoying that we would have to be in the gym at 6 a.m. If we were -1 for the last three holes, we would get a credit. That meant if we were ever over par on the last three holes, the 6 a.m. cardio session would go away. If somebody shot in the 80s, they had to do what was called a "House of Pain": a 6 a.m. cardio session that was pretty intense. We got a House of Pain credit if we shot -2 for the last three holes. I never had an issue with the rule of shooting in the 80s. Division I golfers shouldn't be shooting in the 80s and it embodies the whole round. A running tally of this was recorded and, at the end of the fall season, we would either have to wake up early a few times or be in the clear. For example, if I was over par three times on the last three holes throughout the season and was never under par for the last three holes then I would have to go to the gym at 6 a.m. three times. I had a big issue with the last three holes rule because it was putting extra weight on those holes. What's so special about the last three holes? It's not like a birdie on the seventeenth hole counts for more than a birdie on the fifth hole. The irrationality of this rule really bothered me and I told my coach quite often how it was a really stupid rule that made no logical sense. Here is why: I shot 73 on one round in a qualifier, but I was +1 on the last three holes. One of my team-mates shot 79 but was -2 on the last three holes. He was rewarded with a workout credit and I was punished. How does that make any sense? I beat this kid by six shots and he was rewarded while I got punished. My coach's rationale was that he wanted to get us to feel uncomfortable or attempt to simulate tournament pres-sure by having those holes mean something of value or potential loss. Maybe some of my teammates thought it was good, but I can only speak for myself, and I certainly didn't feel that way.

I understand that sometimes a golfer needs to make a birdie on the last hole or down the stretch to make something happen, but my point is that there are definitely other moments through-out the tournament where a golfer could have done something better. This would eliminate the need to produce magic at the very end. For example, let's say a golfer made a double bogey on the seventh hole of the first day. If he parred that hole, then he wouldn't necessarily need a birdie on the last. But commentators love to focus on the last few holes or on Sunday's round, when in reality they are all the same.

Golf commentators will associate nearly every single bad shot a pro golfer hits on Sunday to nerves. Every bad shot must have been the causation of nerves even though commentators have no idea what a player is feeling or thinking. They will automatically say, "It was nerves." It makes me viscerally ill to hear this. I have to turn the television on mute half the time I watch golf because I don't feel like listening to them spew their ignorance. For example, at the 2014 Deutsche Bank Championship, Billy Horschel chunked his approach shot on the seventy-second hole in the water. He said it was not because of nerves or a choke, it was just an untimely swing. A few days after I heard Johnny Miller say something along the lines of, "I don't believe it had nothing to do with nerves." Miller had absolutely no right to comment on how Horschel felt. Was he in his body and mind? NO. So who is he to say whether he hit a bad shot because of nerves or not more so than the actual person. But that is the way these commentators talk. Every single bad moment is caused by nerves.

To provide some support, here's an example of the commentary from the final round of the 2016 Sony Open. Let me first give you some background on the leaders coming down the stretch: there was Brandt Snedeker, who is a multiple winner on

Tour; Fabian Gomez, who won once his rookie year and was in his second year on Tour; Zac Blair, also in his second year on Tour; and Kevin Kisner—one of the hottest players on the planet at the time—was a shot behind the lead of Snedeker and Blair after fifty-four holes. The Golf Channel hosts discussed during the pregame before the final round how Snedeker and Kisner had an advantage over Blair because they were more "experienced" than he was and would therefore be more comfortable.

As for the round itself, here's how the commentary played out throughout the round. Immediately after Blair hit a bad shot short-sided on the fourteenth hole, one of the commentators said, "It was nerves." How could the commentator possibly know that? The other commentator then said, "Snedeker has an advantage because he is experienced. He knows he needs to hit the fairways and make birdies." Really?! That's what experience tells you. I'm pretty sure a ten-year-old would know that.

Onto Fabian Gomez. On the sixteenth hole, he hit a bad drive that went into the right rough. The commentator instantly said, "I don't know why he hit driver there, especially when his nerves were on display." I'm not sure how his nerves were on display. Was he wearing a sign that said "I am nervous." His very next shot from the rough was right at the pin, fifteen feet short of the hole. Did his nerves suddenly disappear? There was no mention of nerves on that shot.

I promise you I am not making any of this up. If you were to watch the NBC tapes from the final round of the 2016 Sony Open, you will hear them saying verbatim what I am recounting.

On the eighteenth hole, which is a par-5, Zac Blair was two shots behind the lead. He hit the fairway and then rifled a 275 yard three-wood to ten feet for eagle. While the ball was in the air, Blair exclaims, "Oh my gosh, that is so good!"—then—"Let's fucking go!" Even Mormons curse I guess. He didn't make the putt, which would have put him in a playoff. Notah Begay, who was commentating, immediately said, "It must have been because of nerves." But there is no way Notah Begay knows why Blair missed the putt and the simple matter is maybe it just didn't go in. Blair played a very solid round that day, shooting -3, but he missed the putt on the last hole—so it must have been nerves. And you know what? Blair beat Kisner on the last day by three strokes. How in the world is that possible if Kisner was more "experienced" than him? Just because Blair didn't win the tournament it wasn't necessarily because of nerves or experience. He just came up a little short.[13]

Anyway, the tournament ended up going into a playoff between Fabian Gomez and Brandt Snedeker. The commentators immediately started to say that Snedeker had the advantage because he was more experienced than Gomez. Well, guess what? Gomez won the tournament, beating someone who had more "experience" than him. Riddle me that.

The first thing the commentator asked Gomez after the playoff was how big of a factor were nerves. I mean the guy just shot 62, he probably felt pretty comfortable, which he confirmed in his post round interview. These commentators need to change their tune, because theirs is awful. Say something legitimate or nothing at all.

---

[13] Blair is one of my favorite golfers because in my opinion he embodies the complete opposite of what golf culture is perceived as. He is cocky and supremely confident. I know this because I played a round of golf with him in college. The way that this 5'8", 140-pound person conducts himself exudes confidence. He should be the poster child for golf.

GOLF PSYCHOLOGISTS

Now onto the people I have a true disdain for: golf psychologists. I want to say right off the bat, I have a very negative view of these people. I have seen two mental "experts," read a lot of their books, and listened to their audio tapes. While most of what I'll say will poke holes in their logic and arguments, I will be complimentary if they make valid points. I will use myself as anecdotal evidence at times as it's the only mind I know intimately. I will challenge each theory with my personal rationalization and provide research-based evidence for some that may or may not back up my own opinions. As I stated in the first chapter, the reasons I dislike golf shrinks is they make it seem like what they say is factual and absolutely essential. They provide minimal to no proof behind their theories, throw information at people and want them to blindly accept it because they are the so called "gurus" of the mind. In my opinion, if a golf psychologist wants to be taken seriously they should provide backing to support their theories whether that be scientific articles, studies, statistics, or experiments, though it seems they never do. While most psychology experiments do have limitations, it would be a step in the right direction if golf shrinks used this information to back up their statements. Instead, the majority of their evidence is anecdotal, where they say, "PGA Tour golfer XYZ thinks this way, so should you." Another problem is if there is any deviation from what they say and what you do, they will have you believe that you are doing something wrong. What is really unfortunate is that golf culture has legitimized the industry of golf psychology and validated those working within it as "experts." Last I am critical of these people for personal reasons: they made me feel like there was something wrong with my mind because certain—perfectly natural—thoughts crossed it. They made me believe their advice was the simple answer to my irrationalities.

For the most part here are the common themes of golf psychology in no particular order: play one shot at a time or stay in the present moment; don't think about score or results; have positive thoughts and self-talk; and have a pre-shot routine. It's as if all the golf shrinks got together and came up with a standard list of issues, and in order to cure them you have to do XYZ. They make it seem that there is a simple, uniform solution to each individual's mental issues—which is insane.

THEME 1: PLAY ONE SHOT AT A TIME AND STAY IN THE PRESENT MOMENT

When golf psychologists talk about being present and playing one shot at a time, what they're really referring to is the ability to concentrate and focus on the task at hand. Golfers shouldn't be thinking about task-irrelevant stimuli, which can be internal or external. Examples of external stimuli are people in the crowd, a loud noise in the distance, etc. Examples of internal stimuli are your own thoughts that can range from thinking about bills, a date, or worrying about what others may think of you, etc. Since golf is a self-paced activity—meaning that an individual controls the initiation of the event—sports psychologists believe individuals are more susceptible to task-irrelevant stimuli. Creating a pre-shot routine is one method that has gained popularity to reduce task-ir-relevant stimuli. Overall I agree with this belief; golfers should do their best to focus on the shot at hand. It would be phenomenal if a golfer could eliminate all task-irrelevant stimuli.

What I don't like is that golf shrinks make it sound like you're doomed if your mind drifts from the shot at hand. If you happen to think about a shot on another hole, whether it's in the past or future, they will make you believe something is wrong with your mind. It is very natural for our minds to drift and to think about random things, whether they are golf-related or not. What I think the golf shrinks should say is that it's okay for your mind to drift away from the task at hand, as opposed to my experience where they told me there is something wrong with my mind.

In Chapter 1 of *Golf is a Game of Confidence*, Rotella maintains that if a golfer doesn't stay in the present moment their performance will suffer. He gives a fun analogy of a time he was at a conference talking about how it's difficult to stay in the present during a golf tournament and not think about winning. To prove his point, he asked someone in the audience who he thought was the sexiest person on the planet. The person answered Cindy Crawford. Rotella says hypothetically that Cindy Crawford would sleep with this guy that night, but only if he didn't think about it. The guy said, "That's impossible"—and I totally agree. The point that Rotella was trying to make was that this is what golf tournaments are like for PGA Tour pros and that thinking of winning a tournament is a major no-no. To quote from the book:

"To play golf as well as he can, a player has to focus his mind tightly on the shot he is playing now in the present. If the golfer thinks about anything else, that pure reaction between the eye and the brain and the nervous system is polluted. Performance usually suffers. This is just the way human beings are constructed."

My issue with statements such as these is that I don't think it's right to make such a rigid statement about a subjective matter. Again, according to him, "This is just the way human beings are constructed"—there is no room for variation.

THEME 2: DON'T THINK ABOUT RESULTS

One of the main concepts taught by golf shrinks is that a golfer should never think about score or results. They reason that if a golfer thinks about results, it will adversely affect their ability to score and potentially cause anxiety. However, I believe that people can be very motivated to play when thinking about a score. I have often heard golfers pick scores or give themselves goals of a score to shoot. When Jack Nicklaus entered the 1986 Masters final round he was four shots back of the lead. In highlight tapes where Nicklaus discusses his final round, he states that he had a goal of shooting 64 because he felt that was the number he needed to shoot to win. In Tiger's 1997 Masters highlight reel, he also says that he had a goal of shooting even par in Amen Corner[14] during the final round. Additionally, Jordan Spieth told a commentator after the second round of the 2015 British Open, when he was five shots back of the lead, that he had a goal of shooting ten under on the weekend (he ended up missing a playoff by one stroke). It just goes to show how three of the best contradict what many golf psychologists advise. Another notable mental coach, Jim Fannin,

---

[14] Holes 11-13 at the Augusta National.

believes that golfers should have mini goals that consist of target scores every three holes, such as wanting to be -1 on holes 10-12. This runs counter to what Rotella and many other shrinks recommend, which I find amusing. So who is right and who is wrong? **There is no right or wrong**.

I want to give a personal example of how thinking about score helped me play one of the best rounds of my life. I was trying to qualify for the US Amateur in the summer of 2010. I had a poor first round and shot 75. I was seven strokes off the lead. That night at my hotel I came to a realization that the only way I was going to qualify was if I did something legendary the next day. I figured I needed to shoot 64 the following day to qualify. All I was thinking about the next day was that I had to shoot 64. Anything else was a failure because I wouldn't qualify. I was mentally great that day and never nervous. When I got to -2 or -3, I knew I needed to go lower and wanted more birdies. I would have generally become nervous, but not this day. I would yell at myself, "You have to shoot 64, you don't have time to get nervous, you have to keep going lower!" Although I didn't reach my target—I shot 66—it was one of my best tournament rounds. Most golf psychologists would say that is not the way to play optimal golf, but who are they to say what I did was wrong?

I saw my first sports psychologist at thirteen, Dr. BS. Calling him "Dr. BS" should give you an idea of how much respect I have for him. The first half of the day took place in a classroom setting where he discussed the typical mental mumbo jumbo, such as don't think about score, think positively, etc. The second part of the day was on the golf course. His goal for me was to think about the process and pre-shot routine. If I ever thought about score or the value of a putt, such as "this is a birdie putt," then I had to put an object in my golf bag. I was constantly putting objects in my bag during the round with Dr. BS. I told him that the thought of a putt being for certain scores was entering my mind—and consequently continually filling my bag since I had such thoughts. My dad had accompanied me on this session and I overheard him ask Dr. BS how I was doing/ if I was getting better. Dr. BS said something along the lines that I had a lot of objects in my bag so still not quite getting it. It was blatantly wrong of Dr. BS to tell me that something was mentally wrong with me because I thought about score. It's very difficult for a golfer to not know how they stand throughout the round and the bottom line is that it's not a bad thing like he made me believe. I believe it's impossible to have such mental control and not think about something so prevalent such as your score in a golf round. It's just not realistic human behavior. But how was I supposed to know that Dr. BS was feeding me complete garbage. I was a kid and he was a psychology "expert," so I figured something was wrong with me since he told me good golfers don't think about score.

In Chapter 2 of *The Unstoppable Golfer*, Rotella talks about taking pride in the process more than outcome: "The more important question is not how many strokes you took but whether you went through your mental and physical routine on every shot, whether you had your mind where you wanted it to be before every swing." Mr. O preaches the same thing. That's why he wants his clients to record in their journals the percentage of times they ran their mental program along with their score. This is so soft to me. Can you imagine a PGA Tour player saying the following after missing multiple cuts? "I am really pleased about the last few weeks since I have been executing my pre-shot routine and doing the process well." That is like a CEO saying "We lost millions of dollars in revenue, our costs went up, we lost hundreds of clients, and our stock price is down 25 percent this quarter. But you know what, I did the process of trying to do those things well so it's okay." Let's get one thing straight, in golf, as in everything else in life, the only thing that matters is results (as long as you're acting in an ethical manner).

Similarly, I often hear golfers talk about how a bad golf round is not that big a deal. I agree that a golfer should not dwell on a bad round and move on quickly, but it is a big deal. I heard Bubba Watson say on Feherty how golf is not very important in the end, but he's wrong. Maybe it's not as important to him because he has already achieved so much success. But tell that to a mini tour player who must play well to get through Q-School or to make enough money to play in another tournament. How he/she plays is unbelievably important. Jack Nicklaus said it well in another Feherty interview, "Golf is very important, we wouldn't be here talking right now if it was not for golf."

THEME 3: THINK/TALK POSITIVELY

For this argument I am solely going to provide my own rationale. The reasoning for this is that the experiments I read had too many limitations and, in my opinion, the results couldn't be taken seriously whether they supported or discredited my claim. These limitations include having the participants determine their own stress levels, either through introspection or questionnaires. Making subjects aware of the experiment which inherently polluted the validity of the experiment. Lastly, there had to be instances of unreliable data collection, with there likely being a significant amount of data that went unrecorded due to the fact that the experimenters can't measure every thought a subject thinks. Without further ado, my two cents on the subject.

Positive thinking might be the most ridiculous thing I have ever heard. Golf psychologists will have you believe that the reason PGA Tour golfers are good at golf is because they think positively and that every good shot is the causation of a caddie uttering positive words. For example, in scenarios where psychologists describe conversations between caddies and players, if a caddie says something like, "Okay, now get a good image, make a good swing, and trust it," the psychologist will get excited and say, "Wow, what great words by the caddie!" and give some of the credit to the caddie for the good shot. They will, in fact, try to make it seem that the causation of the good shot was the caddie's words and not that an incredibly talented PGA Tour player hit the shot. Here is one of countless counterexamples to that. At the 2016 Valspar Championship, I watched the group of Erik Compton, Patrick Rodgers, and Lucas Glover—something I wanted to do as I know Erik a little and played a few rounds with Rodgers in college. During the round, Rodgers had a four-footer for birdie straight uphill on a hole and his caddie said, "Make a good stroke." Guess what? He missed the putt. How in the world could a golfer hit a bad shot or putt if the caddie gave his player such "positive imagery"? Shrinks need to stop trying to make it seem that positivity is the causation of good shots.

Here are some of my personal arguments as to why positive thinking is completely absurd. When a person is good at something or something is natural they don't need to think "positively." For instance, when someone eats dinner do they need to say, "Oh, I am really good at piercing the food with my fork, elevating it toward my mouth, chewing it, and then swallowing it." Or how about someone brushing their teeth, "It's incredible how good I am at putting toothpaste on the brush; I brush my teeth really well, I get all the way back and clean my molars incredibly. I might be the best in the world at brushing my teeth." I mean how ridiculous does that sound! That's the way psychologists want you to talk to yourself in golf. But there is no need for positive talk. You shouldn't have to "think positive" in golf just like you don't have to "think positive" to eat or brush your teeth. You just do it. If you had to speculate, do you think a caveman thought positively when he was spearing a wild animal? Hell no! He just grunted and speared that thing. There is no need for positive thinking. Positive thinking might be one of the most ludicrous things I have ever heard. Yet the golf shrinks think it's the Holy Grail, the cure to cancer, and the solution to America's debt.

Some of these "mental gurus" will go so far as to say that even hearing or seeing negative things will affect you. For example, Mr. O told me hearing people talk about their bad rounds or shots will hurt my "self-image" and make me worse. Additionally, seeing people miss putts or seeing somebody shank a shot would have the same effect. I never had an issue with any of that up until I saw him. The only thing that bothered me was hearing people talk about their rounds because I had no interest. But after I saw him, I would avoid talking to golfers because I didn't want to hurt my golf game by hearing about other players' bad golf shots. I also stopped watching golfers who had short putts because I was afraid if I saw a miss, it would make me miss. You know what the inherent problem with what Mr. O said is? A person cannot live their life in a box, trying to hear no evil, see no evil, and speak no evil. You cannot control what people say, what they do, or what kind of shots they hit. This can be said with anything in life. After I got older and matured, I realized the flaws in his theories and I am unaffected by what people do now. It's not like the sky is going to fall down if you are surrounded by some negativity or if you say something negative.

On a similar note to positive thinking is body language. I have heard how a golfer must "walk like a champion" to play their best. Jim Fannin is a big proponent of this theory. What shrinks mean by good body language, is having your chest out and chin up. Well, let me ask you this, does Jason Dufner walk like a champion? Maybe he does and the golf psychologists have just made up another theory as to how golfers should walk based on nothing. Clearly Dufner doesn't walk how the shrinks say someone should, yet he has had an incredibly successful PGA Tour career. Jim Fannin goes so far as to say that a person should never have their head down because if your head is down you are susceptible to negative thinking. In other words, if your head is up you are less likely to think negatively. He doesn't base this on any evidence and admits he cannot find the answer to this claim.

In Chapter 2 of *The Unstoppable Golfer*, Rotella talks about training your mind at night by giving it positive imagery. Mr. O and Fannin say essentially the same thing when they suggest people should imprint good memories in their mind. Rotella maintains the importance of both physical and mental training: a golfer should incorporate time in the day or at night to visualize success because that can be as important as physical practice. One way to test this is by creating two groups of beginner golfers and have one group do physical practice and the other practice solely in their mind, then collect data from the performance of both groups to determine which has a more powerful effect. This would at least be a step in the right direction to see if there is any support to that claim. While I agree that beating balls all day doesn't necessarily translate to success, I think it's farfetched to think that visualizing good swings and putts is really going to help.

On a similar note, in Chapter 9 of *Your 15th Club*, Rotella starts to talk about visualization. How if you see yourself doing things your subconscious doesn't know the difference between reality and imagination. According to many shrinks, a golfer will be better prepared for positive performance if they visualize them happening. The likelihood of such events occurring also increases if you visualize them. Let me tell you something: I have been visualizing dating Jennifer Anniston for many years and, unfortunately, it still hasn't happened and all the visualization in the world wouldn't prepare me for it.

Rotella states in *Your 15th Club*—as he does in many books—that confidence is a choice. On a similar note, in Chapter 14 of *Golf is Not a Game of Perfect*, Rotella talks about free will and that a golfer can think any way they so choose. I have to admit there have been times when I almost willed myself into making birdies, but I think it is ridiculous to say that confidence is a choice. If it was a choice, why wouldn't I choose to be confident when one of my anxiety triggers presented itself? If I could choose to not have fear in front of my older college teammates or coach, don't you think I would? But I would get certain fearful symptoms, such as physical shaking, in their presence which was not really in my control or my free will. My point is that my anxiety or fear was so pervasive that I could not "choose" to be confident or calm. Sports psychologists have presented techniques to calm down, such as Jim Fannin's "rebooting" that consists of deep breathing and visualization. However, all of these mental tricks, whether you want to call it a "reboot" or some other fancy name, never did anything for me when I was anxious on the golf course. While I wholeheartedly agree with Rotella that confidence is a very big key to success, I don't agree with golf psychologists ways of getting it. I don't have the answer to that and I don't think anyone does. It's a very individualistic attribute. That is what I dislike about these shrinks. They make it seem like they have all the answers on how to gain confidence and that their methods are proven. Nobody can prove many matters of the brain. Many topics are too mysterious and unmeasurable.

In Chapter 4 of *Your 15th Club*, Rotella even says it himself that some topics are unprovable or nebulous. To quote, "So as I begin to talk about terms like the conscious mind, the subconscious mind, and the self-image, keep in mind that these are not tangible things like pistons, spark plugs, and carburetors. I know they exist within us. But ultimately I know it as a matter of faith." To be fair, Rotella does provide these types of disclaimers throughout his books which I do appreciate.

In Chapter 11 of the same book he discusses self-talk and how if people say things like, "I am the greatest," or "I am the US Open champ," then they will be better mentally and have a better self-image. If you say things like, "I suck," then you will suck. I just can't agree with this. Although I agree it's not good to dwell on negativity or beat yourself up, saying you suck every once in a while is not that big of a deal. In fact, talking negatively can be motivational. It just depends on how the individual internalizes the thought. Here is an example. In the third or fourth round of the 2017 John Deere Classic, Zach Johnson got a bit upset with himself on the seventeenth hole for running a putt past the hole. Gary McCord made the comment how sports psychologists would say a golfer should talk positively to themselves no matter how bad things are going. He then started to have a conversation with Dottie Pepper and asked if she berated herself in a positive or negative tone. Dottie said, "I stayed true to myself and berated myself negatively." This contradicts what shrinks would say but it obviously worked for her since she won seventeen LPGA events. The world is not going to end if you talk negatively. But according to the golf shrinks, just by uttering the words "I suck," you will hurt your self-image, your self-confidence, you will go bald, lose an arm, and other terrible things will happen. It's just so preposterous.

Another topic that falls under positive thinking is having a mantra where a person says what they want to become. According to psychologists, mantras can help people become that person. As I stated earlier in the book: mantras did nothing for me.

My final thought on this topic is that it's inherently unnatural to think about self-confidence or to forcefully think positively. A golfer should just go about their round or practice and let it be. Most shrinks want their clients to feed their mind and work on their mental game by feeding it positive imagery. This is very bizarre and unnatural to me. It's like thinking about thinking.

THEME 4: HAVE A PRE-SHOT ROUTINE

According to the golf shrinks, if you have a pre-shot routine it should be impossible to think about anything else besides the task at hand, it should improve performance and be a calming influence. I would first like to give my personal opinion on the matter before describing the results from a few studies that touch on the subject.

I have to agree with the fact that having a pre-shot routine and trying to do the same thing repeatedly is very helpful with alignment and things of that nature. But, according to Mr. O, the conscious mind is incapable of thinking of more than one thing at a time. A really big part of his program is how the pre-shot routine occupies a golfer's mind so that they cannot think of anything else. Most golf shrinks would agree with this theory for self-paced sports. Maybe it's true that the mind can only think about one thing at a time but that doesn't mean that it cannot bounce around and think about different topics. My experience with golf shrinks is that if you ever stray from your routine or if you have an intrusive thought, they will have you believe that there is something wrong with you.

Golf shrinks also say if you do your pre-shot routine it will help you remain calm because you are not thinking about the importance of the situation. Let me tell you something, when one of my anxiety triggers showed up, my pre-shot routine didn't calm me down—nothing short of a tranquilizer dart was going to settle me.

An article, *The Pre-shot Routine: A Prerequisite for Successful Performance?*, by Robin Jackson of Brunel University concludes that there is no evidence that implies performing your routine consistently will lead to improved performance. Jackson briefly touches on a few experiments that make that claim but the results are the same. There is plenty of anecdotal evidence that elite golfers have well-structured pre-shot routines.[15] But the question is if that leads to superior performance. There have been studies showing that lower handicap golfers adhere to their predominant routines more consistently than higher handicappers. A study by Thomas and Over (1994) sampled 165 club golfers with handicaps ranging from five to twenty-seven and found that lower handicap golfers adhered to their routines more consistently than higher handicappers. However, it cannot be inferred that routine consistency led to superior performance.

I would like to discuss in detail one experiment that touches on the subject. The study observed three male DI collegiate golfers and set out to determine the percentage of times the subjects performed their pre-shot routines successfully. In order to determine a successful routine completion, the experimenters interviewed the subjects to determine their mental and physical routines. For example, a subject could describe his physical routine as something along these lines:

1. Select club
2. Stand behind the ball
3. Take deep breath
4. Place club behind ball
5. Set feet
6. Take one look at target
7. Swing

---

[15] The article *The Experience of Preshot Routines among Professional Golfers: An Existential Phenomenological Investigation* illustrates this anecdotal evidence.

The observers then videotaped the subjects to determine if the physical routine was performed correctly and gave each sample a score of either "completed" or "not completed" based on what the subjects said their routines were. This determined a baseline for the percentage of times each subject followed their pre-shot routine. To determine if mental routines were followed, subjects were interviewed post round and went through checklists to see if they followed what they described as their mental routine. At different time periods in the study, the experimenter performed an intervention on the subjects to teach them how to consistently align, make a decisive decision and be totally committed to each shot. This intervention was referred to as the "treatment." The treatment was administered at different times to each subject so that if an increase in pre-shot routine consistency was achieved it could be attributed to the treatment. The results of the experiment show that routines were followed more consistently after the treatment for all three subjects. This included mental and physical routines. However, this didn't immediately lead to improved performance from a scoring standpoint. In a follow-up completed four months after the experiment, the subjects showed an improvement in scoring, though it cannot be inferred that routine consistency was the reasoning. To quote from the study, "Results must be viewed with caution because it is difficult to determine what factors were responsible for improved performance: physical practice, cognitive-behavioral intervention, a combination of both, or unknown variables." The experimenters admit the waters are too murky to conclude that pre-shot routine was the determinant for improved performance. There are other factors that could also have led to the lower scoring. For example, the weather could have been better in the follow-up, the pin positions could have been friendlier, or perhaps the greens were more receptive.

If you read the study, you can tell that the experimenters were pleased that the subjects' routine consistency increased. But I thought to myself, "Who really cares about the experiment if it cannot be concluded that consistently executed routines lead to improved performance?" Let's throw a party now that the subjects follow their routines more consistently! Whoopee-doo! The one minor takeaway is that the subjects describe that they felt mental improvements. The reason I use the words "minor takeaway" is because this cannot be measured and it relies on introspection, which—if you recall Wilhelm Wundt's methods of experimentation—is subjective evidence.

By the way, who do you think did this experiment? Dr. Bob Rotella, and his colleagues at the University of Virginia.

This is my opinion on pre-shot routines: a golfer shouldn't hold their breath thinking that a more structured pre-shot routine is going to lower their scores. I know a major reason golf shrinks are proponents of physical and mental routines is they claim that the mind will be less distracted by task-irrelevant stimuli. But I think it depends on the individual. For some people a strong routine may make all the difference in the world, yet it may not for others. It did not help me.

Yes, great golfers have their routines but that cannot be attributed as the cause of their success. There is a big difference between correlation and causation. Let me put it to you this way, you can create a routine for just about anything in life. Let's say I want to create a routine for tying my shoes every morning. Let's go step by step:

1. Place my shoes on the ground
2. Place my right foot in my right shoe, followed by placing my left foot in my left shoe
3. Take a deep breath
4. Say the trigger words "loop, swoop, and pull"
5. Grab the shoe laces and start tying
6. Adjust feet so they are comfortably resting in the shoe

At the end of the day you are going to be tying your shoes whether you do the routine or not. My point is that you are still going to be a good or bad golfer whether you perform your routine perfectly to the .000001 second, if you are off by a few seconds, if you forget a step, or deviate from it slightly. If you think that a stronger, more structured routine will help you then by all means incorporate one. It's very individualistic. There isn't a set way of doing it.

MISCELLANEOUS THEMES

Now there are other topics that golf psychologists talk about that I don't think fall under any of the previous themes but I would still like to address them. In a number of books psychologists say how you shouldn't have swing thoughts. Here is a quote from Chapter 3 of *Golf is a Game of Confidence:* "A golfer cannot score as well as possible if he is thinking about his swing mechanics as he plays. Research in sports psychology is only beginning to reveal why this is so. The best I can say is that the human organism performs repetitive physical tasks best if the brain is not consciously trying to guide the process. It performs best when an individual focuses on a target or goal and does not think about how to execute the movement."

I am going to describe two studies that examined whether it's more beneficial to be target-oriented or focused on swing mechanics. The studies refer to swing thoughts as "internal attention" and being target-oriented as "external attention." A study done by Perkins-Ceccato, Passmore, and Lee (2003) examined the influence internal and external attention had on the performance of pitch shots of various distances. Performance was measured by the landing proximity of a golf ball to a pylon, which was the target. There were two groups in the experiment: one consisted of ten golfers whose mean handicap was 4 with a range of 0 to 8 and the other of ten golfers with a mean handicap of 26 with a range of 20 to 36. The groups rotated what they focused on for each set of shots. For instance, for the internal attention set of shots, subjects were told to focus on the form of their swing and adjust the force of the swing depending on the distance of the pitch shot. On the external set of shots, the group was told to focus on putting the ball as close as possible to the target. The results showed that the higher skilled golfers performed better with external attention and the lower skilled group performed better with internal attention on mechanics.

A similar study by Wulf and Su (2007) examined five expert golfers who were members of the University of Nevada Las Vegas men's golf team and an individual with an 8-handicap. They performed a similar experiment to the one just described. The subjects rotated what they focused on, whether that be internal awareness, external focus, or no attentional focus (control conditions). The thoughts were slightly different between the two experiments. In this experiment the instructions for the internal focus group was directed at the swinging motion of the arms. The external focus participants were told to focus on the pendulum-like motion of the club, while participants in the control condition were free to focus on what they typically focused on. The results from this experiment were similar to Perkins-Ceccato, Passmore, and Lee's study: expert golfers perform better when their attention is external, meaning not focused on the movement of their body.

Even though these experiments provide evidence that external focus leads to better performance, it's not as if that puts a nail in the coffin and there is no more room for debate. There are limitations to the experiments, such as the small sample size in terms of the number of shots and people observed, and that only pitch shots were examined. In addition, who knows what the subjects were even thinking despite being put in a certain group. I will play devil's advocate to myself and say that a majority of research demonstrates that being target-oriented does seem to lead to improved performance. But that doesn't mean it is set in stone.

I would like to give a personal example of when having my attention on swing mechanics led to a great performance. I won my first full-field college event my senior year of school. I shot 68-71-68. I have never hit the ball so well in my life. I was an absolute machine that week. My swing thoughts were part of the reason I was such a machine: "Right pocket back, elbows, down the toe line, and alligator arms." These thoughts were technical positions that I tried to achieve on every swing. Nobody in the world can tell me that was too many thoughts or that I would have been better off not thinking about my mechanics. It worked for me that tournament and I won. Just because "experts" with PhDs claim this is not the optimal way to swing a golf club doesn't make them right. In Chapter 3 of *Golf is Not a Game of Perfect,* Rotella says, "You cannot hit a golf ball consistently well if you think about the mechanics of your swing as you play." Rotella's response as to the why is, "I cannot give a scientific reply. Psychologists and other specialists in human performance may one day figure it out." Does that sound like a convincing answer?! I have to admit I became pretty upset when I read that paragraph. Here is someone who has become a public figure in the golfing world and so many believe what he says, yet he doesn't provide persuasive evidence to back a majority of his beliefs. So why should anybody believe him if he doesn't provide conclusive support. I have never understood why golf psychologists and instructors have their opinions on swing thoughts. Some say you should have no thoughts. Some say you should have a maximum of one. Some say you should have one on the backswing and one on the downswing. Well, it's a matter of personal preference and you should do what works for you despite the "experts" telling you there is a right or wrong number of swing thoughts. In addition, there might be some days where you like to have swing thoughts and other days where you don't. It doesn't have to be static. You can change the thoughts and the number of thoughts based on what you feel is most beneficial. I have gone through times in my career where I had swing thoughts and others where I did not. **There is no right or wrong.**

Another thing in just about every one of Rotella's books is how he doesn't emphasize the importance of the long game enough. I find this strange considering that he and his fellow researchers concluded in *Predictability and Stability of Professional Golf Association Tour Statistics* (1994) that greens in regulation is most highly associated with low scoring average, followed by driving accuracy, then putts per round. In essence that means if a golfer has a good or bad day of driving and iron play, this will magnify the results far more than if their putting is on or off. So I find it very peculiar that the message in his books is that short game is king when he has found contrary evidence. In Chapter 22 of *The Golfer's Mind* he does a good job of stating that a player must be long enough off the tee to be competitive and sharp with their scoring clubs, which he considers eight iron to wedges to score well. However, he really tries to emphasize the importance of putting more than anything else. For example, "No matter what level you play at you're going to take an average of twenty-seven or more of your strokes with your putter during every round. That's about twice as many as you'll take with any other club. Thus, the fastest way to improve your scores is by improving your putting." In addition, he wrote a book that was solely dedicated to putting. I am not saying that putting is unimportant and that the long game is all that matters—I would be an absolute idiot if I said that. He has, in my opinion, a very old school way of thinking with the "drive for show, putt for dough" mentality. The game of golf is becoming more of a power game. You can't say that Dustin Johnson, Bubba Watson, Brooks Koepka, and Gary Woodland don't have an incredible advantage over shorter hitters. Obviously there are golfers, such as Zach Johnson or Jim Furyk, who don't bomb it and are still the best in the world. But his overall message is that it doesn't matter how you hit the ball as long as you keep it in play and make up and downs. As Lee Trevino once said, "There are two things that will not last long in this world, and that's dogs chasing cars, and pros putting for pars."

Further evidence that contradicts this common belief that putting and short game are the most important ways to improve scoring is the book *Every Shot Counts* by Mark Broadie. He debunks many commonly accepted schools of thought that have polluted the game. His book provides statistical evidence on how the long game is of greater importance than the short game to improving scores for both amateurs and pros. Besides a few exceptions, the more the average Tour player and amateur can improve their long game, the more their scores will drop. All of this is backed up with a huge sample size of data consisting of hundreds of tournaments, thousands of rounds, and millions of shots provided by Shotlink.[16] New statistics over the last few years have also validated that driving distance and accuracy, proximity to hole, and other ball striking metrics can really help improve scores, all thanks to Professor Broadie. What I love about Broadie's book is that he uses hard data, numbers, and facts—which

---

[16] For those of you who don't know what Shotlink is, it's the Tour's proprietary real-time scoring system that captures multiple data points on every shot struck during competition, which in turn translates into thousands of statistics.

you can't ignore—to make his claims. As he says, academics would call his data collection "robust results."

In Chapter 6 of *Golf is Not a Game of Perfect*, Rotella uses Sam Snead as an example of overcomplicating one's swing. Rotella says that when Snead turned professional in the early 1930s, he convinced himself that the way he learned to play golf in a pasture with whittled sticks in the shape of clubs and not thinking wasn't good enough for professional competition. Well the same argument can be said about golf psychology this day and age. People are doing enough without having a sports psychologist. But nowadays golfers might think they need to incorporate psychology just like Snead thought he needed to concentrate or think more for professional golf. Golf psychology has overcomplicated the mind and filled golf with so many dos and don'ts that are based on untrustworthy evidence.

Another person whose material I have read is Jim Fannin. I have listened to some of his audio tapes and read his book *The Pebble in the Shoe*. Here are some of the key points he makes: He says that the average person has 2,000 to 4,000 thoughts a day. He then goes on to say that world champion athletes only have 1,100 thoughts a day. According to him they have eliminated thoughts of impatience, frustration, embarrassment, jealousy, envy, worry, anxiety, gossip, rumor, hearsay, and assumptions. I will agree that it would be ideal if someone could eliminate those thoughts. But it's tough for me to accept that just because someone is a successful pro athlete they somehow have totally eliminated those thoughts. They are human beings like anyone else. My biggest question is where did he get those numbers from? Dr. BS has material where he says that people have 66,000 thoughts a day. Now the difference between 4,000 and 66,000 thoughts isn't a small one. So who is right and who is wrong? Maybe they are both wrong and need to clearly define what they consider a "thought." Do they consider a "thought" to be a conscious thought or do they consider a "thought" something that triggers involuntary actions such as breathing or me moving my fingers to type this book? They don't clarify this and are essentially pushing numbers on you about something that can't be quantified.

Something that I noticed in my research on golf psychologists is that they display a logical fallacy known as confirmation bias.[17] They will essentially use the result of specific instances as proof for their theories even if their beliefs are not the true reason as to why an event occurred. For example, a person might say, "I believe the sun is going to rise today." Then when the sun rises, the individual attributes the rising sun to the fact that he "believed" that the sun was going to rise and not the true reasoning which, of course, is the earth's rotation.

Here are some examples of what I am referring to. In Chapter 6 of *The Golfer's Mind*, Rotella tells a story about a mini tour player who was playing really well before he attempted to do a Monday qualifier for a PGA Tour event. He states how this player was playing superbly, winning a few events before the qualifier. The mini tour player even told his wife he felt so confident that he thought he might win the entire PGA Tour event. Rotella describes how his client told

---

[17] Confirmation bias is the tendency to interpret new evidence as confirmation of one's existing beliefs or theories.

his wife that he played "tight and scared." Rotella proclaims that he knew immediately what had happened to the mini tour player: "On the mini tours, the client was not particularly concerned about the results. He focused on his pre-shot routine, on making each shot a quality shot. [...] When he stepped off the mini tour, he forgot about that. He started thinking about the future, as evidenced by the fact that he told his wife he thought he might win the whole tournament. Consequently, with his mind not in the present, he played tight and scared and badly."

If this mini tour player had qualified for the event and had a respectable finish Rotella would be singing a totally different tune. He most likely would be saying how the mini tour player performed well because his self-image was that he was going to win the tournament or that he was extremely confident. However, the concept that Rotella is trying to emphasize in this section is "staying in the present," so he uses this story as evidence that thinking in the future will lead to bad performance, even though it might not have been the true cause.

He displays confirmation bias once again in the book *Golf is a Game of Confidence.* He uses the outcome of his client, Brad Faxon, in an attempt to provide support for his theories. He attributes whatever Faxon does well to the point he is trying to make. On the flip side, if Faxon missed a shot he attributes it to the fact that he disobeyed whatever point he is trying to make. For example, Rotella describes Faxon's final round in the 1995 PGA Championship. He tells stories such as how on the eighth hole he had an eight-footer for birdie, he was doing well in the round, and the crowd was going crazy. So Rotella says, "Distractions were assaulting Brad's mind. He thought that making the putt would move him to seven under for the day, and perhaps into the tournament's top five. Not coincidentally, for the first time that day, he overread a putt. He played a break that wasn't there, and the ball slid by the hole." I can just about guarantee if that putt went in, the writing in that book would have changed. He would be saying how Faxon believed in himself or something just to prove his point. Later in that same story, Rotella talks about how he wants his players to embrace nervous symptoms. So on the ninth hole Faxon made a twenty-five-footer for birdie and Rotella says, "Brad welcomed his symptoms . . . [and made the birdie putt.]" Had he not hit such a great putt it's safe to assume that Rotella would probably be saying he didn't embrace his nervous symptoms. I wanted to highlight these stories because it shows how Rotella interprets events in a biased manner in order to confirm the theories he seeks to support. In the examples above, it is staying in the present and embracing nerves.

I will end the chapter talking about parts of a book I like, *Zen Golf* by Dr. Joseph Parent, which has some tips that I believe are less rigid and more helpful than the previously mentioned theories. In Part I of the book he says how a person "is not their thoughts." He tells a story about a student who tells his master that he has trouble controlling his mind. How the thoughts he wants to stay, leave, and the ones he does not want end up staying. The master tells the student the mind is like a horse, it will fight back if you try to control it. But if you just let the horse run around in a field, it will eventually settle down. I like this story a lot. It contradicts what other shrinks say. It describes how it is impossible to control your mind, which I believe is more realistic. Parent essentially says that it is not that big of a deal if your mind has negative thoughts: "Thoughts arise *in* our mind, but they are *not our* mind." This is in opposition to so many golf psychologists that say if a negative thought enters your mind you are doomed to hit a bad golf shot. A few pages later in the book he says, "As thoughts arise, you simply let them come up and go by, neither inviting them to stay nor trying to get rid of them. Noticing them is enough; there's no need for analyzing or judging them." I really like this since I believe you have no control of your thoughts. You should not freak out when you have a negative thought. The same can be said for a positive thought. Just because you feel like you're the greatest doesn't make it so. These are just thoughts; they hold no power or meaning. They are like leaves in the wind and you should let them come and go. This type of thinking reminds me of Dr. L, the regular psychologist I saw in Colorado, and how she told me just to accept the fact that I will have random thoughts. Later in the book Parent acknowledges that you shouldn't fight last minute thoughts that can occur right before you hit a golf shot. This is a direct counterexample to Mr. O, who says if you do your routine you will never have random thoughts. Parent says don't freak out about thoughts just let them come and go—which is far more natural.

Later on in the book he talks about how golfers who meditate or do mindfulness exercises want to "clear their minds." He observes, "[People who meditate] become frustrated because they don't seem to be able to stop their thoughts. This is based on misconception about presence, clarity of mind, and meditation. They think the goal is to be able to make their mind go blank. Unless you're unconscious, that doesn't happen. Your mind will always be full of the contents of awareness, and often those contents will be thoughts." TM is very similar to this. TM says the occurrence of random thoughts is natural. Although I don't agree with most of what TM preaches, both TM and Parent stress the point that you don't have complete control of your mind. I love what Parent says. He has a different view from the golf psychologists who say that negative thoughts are the end of the world.

Now I do not agree with everything that Parent says, such as needing to walk with good posture, that you need a certain level of intensity to perform at your best, or not having swing thoughts. But I will give him a pass and not critique him as most of what he says is logical to me.

I would like to conclude with the following thought regarding the various psychological theories I was either exposed to or read about. For the most part, for something to be considered scientifically rigorous it needs to meet certain requirements. A short list of this includes quantifiable measurements, controlled experimentation, reproducibility, predictability, and testability. Now ask yourself: Do any of the theories I described sound like they can meet that scientific burden of proof? There is no way to quantify how confident a golfer is, if a pre-shot routine improves performance, or how many thoughts a person has. It is impossible to replicate situations where a specific golfer would feel the exact same emotions, confidence, anxiety, and numerous other factors. The points of reference are impossible to reproduce. That is what makes sports psychology so mysterious and difficult to test, and why it ultimately can't be proven (the reason for my distrust for the profession). Due to sports psychologists' flaws in logic, fallacious reasoning, and lack of evidence people should be very cautious of the information that is presented to them. Lastly, golfers need to make up their own minds as to what is beneficial to them despite what anybody says. **There is no right or wrong.**

JASON BURSTYN

CHAPTER 5

What If I Don't Make It?/Pro Golf

In this chapter I want to shed some light on the life of professional golf. Although this does not have to do with the main theme of the book, it is still something I would like to educate people about since most people have no idea what pro golf is like. They might be familiar with the PGA Tour and golfers such as Tiger Woods, Vijay Singh, or Adam Scott, but there is a whole other world that is far less glamorous.

I have the most respect for professional golfers because they earn every dollar they make. Someone might say, "Oh, they have endorsements." Let me tell you something the golfers who have really big endorsements got them because they won or were constantly high up on the leaderboard. With other sports, especially basketball and baseball, players are guaranteed their money. It is not a big deal in these sports to have a bad game because the athlete will still get paid. Mike Stanton can strike out every time at bat and he will still get $300 million. Maybe there are details in the contract that I don't know about, but you get the point I am trying to make. While I admire their talent and athletic ability, the fact that they have guaranteed money inherently reduces my level of admiration for them. I am obviously biased because my whole life has been about golf, but the point remains: golfers have skin in the game.

Upon graduating college, a lot of golfers turn pro and give professional golf a shot. Some have absolutely no business doing it and are guaranteed to lose money. Essentially, what professional golf is like at the mini tour level is organized gambling. Players pay their own entry fees and these entry fees create the purse or prize money. The more players that enter a given event, the bigger the purse will be. For example, let's say that I am running a tournament called the Jason Burstyn Invitational with an entry of $100 and ten people sign up. The purse would be $1,000. As the tournament director I decide how the purse should be divided. Perhaps I want to pay the top 33 percent or top 40 percent of the field. So let's say for my theoretical ten-man field I want to pay the top 40 percent, this means that four players will get paychecks and the purse breakdown will be the following: First place $600, second $250, third $100, and fourth $50. As you can see, just because you earn a paycheck, doesn't mean you made money. The guy who came in third place broke even and the guy who came in fourth lost $50. He'd be better off (monetarily) watching TV at home.

However, it's not that simple. When a player enters a tournament, not all of the money goes into the pot. As the tournament organizer, I am going to take a cut of the player's entry fee and I have to pay the golf course as well. So let's say I take $10 from each contestant and pay the golf course $30 greens fees per player. My purse has just shrunk by 40 percent and is now $600 in total. The new breakdown of the purse is as follows: first place $350, second $150, third $75, and fourth $25. You might be saying a $25 check is ridiculous but, believe me, I have gotten plenty of them. This is the typical business model for most mini tours.

But there is still more to it than that. There is a lot of overhead for any given golf tournament. Travel expenses are the biggest costs. Players may have to drive to a golf tournament so they will have gasoline expenses, they may have accommodation expenses, and they have to eat so there are food expenses. Things really get pricy when golfers start to fly to different tournaments as now they have to pay for airfare and they may also have to rent a car. All of these expenses make mini tour life very expensive and not very lucrative. There are different entry fees for different mini tours. For example, I played a lot of mini tour events on the West Florida Golf Tour. The entry fee for a three-day summer event was roughly $450 and the winner got roughly $4,000 if it was a full field event of seventy players. For the most part, this was a low-risk mini tour as I kept my expenses to a minimum. This tour always had its events in the Sarasota/Tampa area, so I moved to Tampa for the summer of 2014. I never had hotel expenses as all the events were within driving distance of my house. On the other hand, there are more expensive mini tours. For example, the Hooter's Tour—or whatever it's called now—is a higher-risk mini tour, meaning they have expensive entry fees. Their entry fees when I was playing were roughly $1,500 but the winner got over $20,000 if it was a full field event. However, these tournaments were scattered around the country so a golfer could never stay in one location. If a golfer were to consistently play on the Hooter's Tour, they would be driving or flying to every tournament and racking up quite the bill.

I will give you a scenario of how much expenses can be at a Hooter's Tour event. Let's say I was living in Tampa and I saw there was a four-day event in the Atlanta area. First off, my entry fee is $1,500. Since I don't want to pay for airfare and rent a car, I will drive to this event. For simplicity we can assume that it will take two tanks of gas to get to Atlanta—so gasoline for a round-trip will cost $160. Then I have to sleep somewhere, so let's say I got a great deal and found a decent three-star hotel for $75 a night. Then, unless I am trying to become a runway model, I need to eat. I will take advantage of the (hopefully) complimentary hotel breakfast; for lunch I will have a turkey sandwich every single day for $7.50, and for dinner I will eat at chains such as TGIF for $15 a night. Since this is a four-day event, I will need a practice round, which will extend my stay to six nights at a hotel. In addition, there most likely will be miscellaneous expenses such as snacks or golf equipment. Let's say that these expenses add up to $50 for the week. Below is a simple spreadsheet to demonstrate the expenses I just described.

HOOTER'S TOUR EVENT EXPENSES	
ENTRY FEE	$1,500
GASOLINE (4 TANKS)	$160
HOTEL (6 NIGHTS)	$450
LUNCH (6X)	$46
DINNER (6X)	$90
MISC.	$50
TOTAL	$2,296

So if this person were to miss the cut he would lose roughly $2,300 for the week. Because of these expenses, mini tour players will do just about anything to cut costs in order to save money. A lot of them have a travel buddy so they can split gasoline and hotel room costs. Some tournaments also try to help out the players by organizing host families that allow players to lodge for free. This is a huge money saver since lodging is one of the biggest expenses. In addition, mini tour players don't live well. They stay in sleazy hotels, crash on friends' couches, and eat crappy food. The amount of Subway that I ate when I was on the mini tours was alarming and today I still don't like to eat it because I ate so much of it while playing professionally.

I was fortunate my parents helped me out. Not that I stayed at the Ritz, but I also didn't stay at roach motels. I also ate decent quality food—I, thankfully, wasn't constantly eating Chicken McNuggets. I have heard of mini tour players sleeping in cars, sleeping on people's floors, and doing absolutely anything to save money.

Because of all the expenses and the low amount of revenue, making money on the mini tours is very difficult. Here are the general measuring sticks of professional golf on the mini tours. If someone is breaking even, they are a pretty good golfer. If someone is able to support themselves, such as pay their rent, car, food, etc., without any sponsorship, then they're good enough to make it. The problem is that there are no guarantees and just because someone is good enough to make it, doesn't mean that they will. What is even sadder to me is when mini tour golfers hemorrhage money and don't move on with their lives.

One of my favorite shows on television is Shark Tank. My favorite person on the show is Kevin O'Leary—or Mr. Wonderful as he likes to call himself—because he is a blunt, straightforward, no non-sense person, and I like that. He often says that if a business is not profitable in three years than it's a hobby and time to move on. I think that is a perfect analogy for golf. If a pro golfer is not profitable after doing nothing else but playing golf all day for three years, then it is time to smell the coffee and move on. If they don't, there is a strong possibility they will be in their thirties, broke, and not have any work experience.

I know this "professional golfer" who has been playing for roughly five years. He mostly does the same mini tour I did in Tampa and regularly shoots in the high 70s. He rarely makes a paycheck and hardly ever makes a cut on a tour where it's not terribly difficult to do so. Yet this person is still at it. I feel in American culture we are taught to never quit, but this person doesn't have a prayer. If anyone looked at his track record there is no indication that he is going to suddenly improve. He is just pissing away money and, in my opinion, that is a crime. Sometimes quitting is the best thing a person can do. To stick with the Shark Tank analogies, on one episode Barbara Corcoran tells an entrepreneur who had a bad business that quitting was probably the best idea. She told a personal story about how she lost $42,000 on a shoe company that she pursued for two years before quitting. She said that quitting that business was the best thing she ever did because after that she started her real estate business and became a real estate tycoon.

As a general rule, it's safe to say that there are no accidents in pro golf. Is it a coincidence that Zach Johnson, Bubba Watson, and Chad Campbell were absolute killers on the Hooter's Tour before making it on Tour? Is it a coincidence that Jon Curran and Ben Silverman killed the Minor League Golf Tour before they made it? Is it a coincidence that Kevin Kisner made over $100,000 on the E-Golf Tour two years in a row before he made it? Is it a coincidence that a ton of golfers on Tour were All-Americans in college? No, no, no, and no. People who are winning tournaments and are very profitable on the mini tours are good enough to make it.

Now what is very difficult is when somebody has proven success and has a legitimate shot at making it but there are no guarantees that person will break through. I will illustrate one of my former teammate's success to prove my point.

He has been playing professional golf for about eight years. He has played in nine Web.com events, where he Monday qualified into six of them, and has one top twenty-five finish. He has played in five PGA Tour events, including the US Open. In those five events he has made two cuts. Additionally, he has won some pretty big mini tour events: the Colorado Open—the second biggest state open— twice, the San Juan Open, and an Adams Tour event. Lastly, he once made it to the final stage of Q-School.

While he is a very accomplished pro golfer, he still has not made it. So I want to make a point to other professional golfers who have not done nearly as much as this person. They should ask themselves, "Have I done anything close to what this person has done in my professional career?" If the answer is "no" after three years, you need to get the hell out of pro golf because you have no business being there.

Now I'm not saying that all mini tour golfers need to be just like this person in order to have a justified reason to keep pursuing pro golf. However, they certainly need to produce some sort of a resume that gives an indication that they have some chance of making it. For example, they might not have won a mini tour event but are consistently in the hunt and finish toward the top of the leaderboard.

What is also difficult is even when someone has made it, there are no guarantees they will stay on Tour. For example, I played a few mini tour events with a guy who was on Tour for two years. He has won a Web.com event and lost in a playoff in a PGA Tour event. Now he is back on the mini tours with essentially no status. He is a great player, but it just goes to show how there are no guarantees in golf. There are no Greg Odens[18] in golf; this would never happen in golf. If a golfer gets injured and can't play, they can't earn. I believe the PGA Tour does have a program where they will pay around $10,000 a month to an injured member. But for the most part, they are not able to make money. This just shows how fickle a sport golf is. Golfers earn every dollar they make. That is why it is the purest sport in my opinion.

On top of the low earning potential, the life of a mini tour player is very nomadic, traveling from place to place, living out of suitcases, and is, in my opinion, pretty brutal. People may think that when somebody is a "professional golfer" they have the coolest job, but if they are not making money, it's the most absurd job in the world. I mean what kind of job is there, other than being a business owner, where someone can very possibly lose money consistently?

I am going to detail my travel schedule after I finished NCAA Regionals to illustrate the nomadic lifestyle of a professional golfer. I played in my first professional golf tournament about a week after

---

[18] For those of you who do not know who Greg Oden is he was the number one NBA draft pick in 2007. While his career was plagued with injuries and he never played a full season, in the NBA players are guaranteed their money—so he got to laugh all the way to the bank.

NCAA Regionals. It was in Riverton, Wyoming, which is about a four-hour drive from Boulder, Colorado. After spending about five days there and collecting a paycheck of $70 (not quite enough to cover expenses), I went back to Boulder. I was so exhausted while driving after the golf tournament that I had to pull over at a rest stop somewhere in Wyoming at around 11:00 at night. I remember closing my eyes at the rest stop trying to sleep, but I could not relax because I was so scared that some hillbilly was going to pop out of nowhere and try to attack me. After about twenty minutes of rest-lessly laying down in my car I got the hell out of there and made it back to Boulder.

After that I took a couple of weeks off, practiced, and played some money games. My next tournament was on June 12 in Wichita, Kansas, for a Web.com Monday qualifier. I drove roughly six hours to play in it. Shot 71(-1) to finish three shots out of a playoff, got in my car and drove right back to Boulder. The next week I drove about seven hours with some of my former teammates to Farmington, New Mexico, for the San Juan Open. About five days after that tournament I drove eight and a half hours from Boulder to Vermillion, South Dakota, to play in a Dakota's Tour event. Since I did not know anybody playing in this event, I did the drive on my own and it was pretty brutal. I was in Vermillion for about five days and my last day of the tourney was interesting. I woke up at roughly 8 a.m., played my round of golf, and shot 72 to earn the last paycheck for $300. After gassing up and eating I believe it was about 4 p.m. I had no intentions of making it back to Boulder that night and figured I would stay at a hotel somewhere on the way. Here are the events that transpired throughout the ride. After about six hours of driving I started to get pretty bored. I had a box of Smart Start cereal with me that I liked to eat so I would stay alert. But munching on cereal didn't help my boredom. It was around midnight when I started going a little crazy. I wasn't tired and was pretty close to Boulder, so I wanted to finish the drive. It suddenly dawned on me as to what I should do. I decided to watch a Youtube video on my phone. So I go onto the website and find the longest video I could on the front page. Now the internet reception in what I think was Sterling, Colorado, was not that great. So I would basically watch a few seconds, pause the video so it could download, all the while continuing to drive, and eat my Smart Start cereal. Definitely not the safest or most traditional way to pass time, but, what can I say, it made the drive a little bit better and I made it back to Boulder around 2 a.m.

After that, I had a few weeks off before I did the Wyoming Open around July 17. This was a nice tournament as it was only about an hour and half from Boulder and I was able to stay at my place some of the nights. It's always a luxury when there is a tournament within driving distance of your residence as it eliminates the need for a hotel. My last tournament before I moved back to Miami was the Colorado Open on July 25th, which was only forty-five minutes away from my place so I didn't need a hotel. After that I drove to my roommate's house in Springfield, Missouri, which was roughly ten hours away, to play in a Web.com qualifier on the 5th of August. Then I made the eighteen-hour journey back to Miami.

When I was in Florida, I didn't travel nearly as much as I did when I was in Boulder. For the most part I played in mini tour events that were in West Palm Beach and Tampa. So I did not rack on the car miles like I did when I was in Boulder. I would say my schedule was on the light side for a pro golfer that summer. When somebody is a pro golfer they are often on the road for as long as a month at a time. I have never done anything like that.

To give you a better idea of what a true journeying professional golfer's schedule is like, I will briefly describe a different pro golfer's schedule. This golfer played on the PGA Tour Latinoamérica and the Canadian Tour. This person already had Latinoamérica status entering the 2014 season. From mid-February to the end of May there were eight events in seven different countries, including Colombia, Mexico, Guatemala, Argentina, Uruguay, Dominican Republic, and Panama. After the last event this person was in the top ten of the money list so was exempt on the Canadian Tour without having to do Q-School. There were a total of seven events in Canada from the end of May till the beginning of August. Then this person started up the Latin American Tour again for the second half of the season which started in the fall. From the end of September till the beginning of December they competed in nine events held in seven different countries including Colombia, Ecuador, Mexico, Peru, Brazil, Chile, and Argentina. I am pretty sure this person played in every single event so at a minimum he was on the road for twenty-four weeks out of the year. If I had to guess it was probably more like thirty-five weeks out of the year, which is around 245 days. Get the picture? It's an absurd amount of traveling. No sport travels like golf does. Like I said I never did anything quite to that extent, but as you can tell, it's a very nomadic lifestyle. Some people may say it's really cool that golfers get to travel the world and see all of these places. There is definitely some truth to that, though I think most golfers on lower level tours would say it's fun but a pretty big grind at the same time. I would say that professional golfers who are truly dedicated to the job are on the road for thirty weeks of the year.

Now that I have talked about the struggles and hardships of being a mini tour player, let me discuss how one "makes it" as a professional golfer. There are a few different ways to advance to the "Turrr." I will start with the most traditional path that most players take to make it which is through Qualifying School or Q-School. This is a lengthy, multi-stage tournament, and if a golfer gets through, they will earn a Web.com Tour card. In the past, a player who made it through Q-School would go straight to the PGA Tour. However, the PGA Tour restructured Q-School in 2013 so that it only gains Web.com status.

So for many golfers, the first step of Q-School is prequalifying, which a player needs to pay roughly $2,500 to enter. When an individual wants to sign up for Q-School, the PGA Tour states the golfer needs to have a certain handicap and a letter from a club pro validating their playing abilities. But in reality, the PGA Tour will gladly take just about anyone's money and it is open to everyone. The real purpose of prequalifying is to weed out golfers who have no business being there. After prequalifying is first-stage. If a golfer started his qualifying process from prequalifying, then he needs to cough up roughly another $2,500 in entrance fees. So on average, depending on the status a golfer has on various professional tours, they need $5,000 to have the right to attempt to qualify for the Web.com Tour. This doesn't include the other expenses such as hotels, gas, food, etc.

Some golfers bypass prequalifying and start the process at first stage. These are the exemptions I know from my playing days that allow a golfer to start at first stage: being a member of the PGA Latinoamérica Tour, PGA Canadian Tour, PGA Tour China, if a golfer has made a cut on these tours or on the Web.com Tour or PGA Tour. So, for instance, my second year of attempting Q-School, I didn't have to play in prequalifying because I was a member of the PGA Latinoamérica Tour.

The process of how a golfer advances through the various stages is more or less the same. A golfer must place high enough in that specific stage in order to advance to the next one. For example, the top thirty places usually get through in first stage. In second stage, approximately the top eighteen get through. If a golfer makes it to third stage of Q-School, which is known as final stage, they automatically have status on the Web.com Tour. Now that may sound great, but just because a golfer has status on a tour doesn't mean they get into tournaments. In order to be guaranteed a spot in tournaments they need to place in approximately the top forty-five out of about 150 golfers. While this may not sound difficult to a lot of people, the golfers who are competing at this stage are great. The players who make it to final stage are pretty damn good.

From there, depending on what place a golfer finishes at in final stage they will earn a different number of guaranteed starts into events. For instance, the winner of Q-School has a high priority ranking and will have a spot in every Web.com event that season without being subject to reshuffles.[19] Whereas a golfer who finished in fortieth place only gets exempt through the first two reshuffles. In order to get more starts, they will need to perform well in events and improve their status. If they don't, they will be subject to a reshuffle which would allow other golfers to take their spots in tournaments. A golfer earns a PGA Tour card if they finish top twenty-five on the money list at the season's end. But there is another opportunity to achieve a Tour card. If a player does not finish inside the top twenty-five, but at twenty-sixth to seventy-fifth, then that player enters what is known as the

---

[19] A reshuffle is conducted after every four regular season events on the Web.com Tour. It essentially rearranges the players who have priority to play in events. Depending on a player's status, they have exemptions in a specific number of events.

"playoffs" with the twenty-five players who earned a Tour card. If a player finishes outside the top seventy-five on the Web.com money list, then they have to repeat the Q-School process. These players who were first to seventy-fifth on the money list compete with the players on the PGA Tour who finished 126th to 200th in FedEx Cup points. These 150 players compete for another twenty-five PGA Tour cards—which I find unbelievably exciting. I find this playoff series more exciting than most golf tournaments.

A lot of professional golfers hate the way Qualifying School has been reorganized in respect to the fact that there is no longer the opportunity to go straight to the PGA Tour. Another knock on the restructuring is that a golfer essentially has worthless status if they make it to final stage but don't finish roughly in the top forty-five. Even then a majority who finish within the top forty-five will have a limited amount of guaranteed tournament starts. I personally do not have an issue with the way the PGA Tour reorganized Q-School in respect to the fact that a player can only get Web.com status. The reorganization certainly did ruin the possibilities of Cinderella stories where a golfer could advance through Q-School and be on Tour despite not doing much beforehand. Success stories like John Huh's are no longer possibile. He had no status on any American tour prior to getting through Q-School and won a PGA Tour event his rookie year. But, as I stated earlier, accidents don't really happen in golf.

What I do have a significant issue with is the price of Qualifying School before and after the reorganization in 2013. Before the restructuring, Q-School cost $5,000 and a golfer had the opportunity to make it to the PGA Tour. So logically, if Q-School only allowed a golfer to earn Web.com status then naturally the price should be cheaper right? EHHHHH . . . wrong! Players still pay the same amount for an inferior product. I'm not saying the Web.com Tour is a bad tour, but it's inferior to the PGA Tour so logically the price should be lower. The reason this occurs is simple economics or the law of supply and demand. Let's put it in terms of a consumer trying to buy a TV. Let's say that the PGA Tour is a nice flat screen TV that costs $5,000 and the Web.com Tour is an old TV set with an antenna coming out of it. Since flat screen TVs are sold out permanently, the store can significantly raise the price of the old TV because there will always be demand. People will always want to watch television and the consumer will be forced to pay the same amount for a second-rate TV. This is the inherent problem with the PGA Tour and the prices they charge for their qualifiers, whether that is Monday qualifiers or Q-School. The PGA Tour is essentially a monopoly; they can set whatever prices they want because they have no competition and constant demand. As a result players will continue to pay exorbitant prices to have the opportunity to qualify for tournaments.

Now Q-School is not the only way to make it to the Web.com Tour. There are tours that are one step below the Web.com Tour just like the Web.com is one step below the PGA Tour. These tours include, PGA Tour China, PGA Tour Latinoamérica, and the Canadian Tour. All of these tours are equivalent to one another. To get on these tours, you must go through Qualifying School as well. Except Q-School, for these tours are only one week instead of multiple weeks for the Web.com. Once a golfer gets his card for one of these tours, if he places first on the money list at season's end he will become a full time member of the Web.com Tour and will not be subject to any reshuffles. There are other very good incentives on these tours as well. For example, if a golfer finishes second through fifth on the money list, they will be exempt for the first four events of the Web.com season before being subjected to the first reshuffle. Or if a golfer finishes sixth to tenth, then he will advance straight to final stage of Web.com Q-School.

There are other untraditional paths besides Q-School to make it to the PGA Tour. For instance, Bud Cauley and Jon Rahm were given sponsor exemptions into PGA Tour events as a result of their high amateur ranking and earned enough prize money to get status on Tour. Tiger Woods was given sponsor exemptions and eventually won the 1996 Las Vegas Invitational, which made him a full member on Tour.

The final way to advance in golf is through Monday qualifiers. A majority of Web.com and PGA Tour events have Monday qualifiers. The way these work is that a golfer can fly out to the city where the Web.com or PGA Tour is playing on any given week and try to qualify. The price of a Monday qualifier for the Web.com is $450 if a player does not have status on any tour. These qualifiers are usually hosted at two sites and six people advance from each site for a total of twelve qualifying spots. In general, if a golfer does not shoot at least -5 they need to pack their bags and get out of town. If a golfer gets through the qualifier on the Web.com, he needs to place in the top twenty-five to get into the tournament the next week. For example, if a player has a solid week and finishes in thirtieth place, he will collect a paycheck but won't have a spot the following week. They will have to Monday qualify again in order to play in another Web.com event.

For the PGA Tour, there is an additional step known as a pre-qualifier that occurs the week before the Monday qualifier. These cost $250.

If a golfer advances through the pre-qualifier, they then advance to the Monday qualifier after paying another $200. An exception to this is that Web.com members and PGA Tour members with partial status only pay $100. In addition, they don't have to go through prequalifying. For PGA Tour Monday qualifiers, a player must place in the top four in order to play in the event. They then need to place top ten in the event to be exempt into the tourney the next week. The only way to become a full member of either tour through a Monday qualifier is to win the tournament. Three golfers who accomplished this feat in PGA Tour events were Fred Wadsworth in 1986, Arjun Atwal in 2010 and most recently Corey Conners in 2019. I know of two golfers on the Web.com Tour who have done it. Ted Potter Jr. in 2011, and Sebastian Cappelen in 2014. Besides winning, if a golfer gets through enough Monday qualifiers and earns enough prize money, they can earn special status on these tours.

Getting through Monday qualifiers is an extremely difficult task. That is why one of the most impressive accomplishments of Patrick Reeds' career was his run with Monday qualifiers, where he got through six qualifiers in 2012.[20] That's an unbelievable achievement.

An additional risk of Monday qualifiers is if a player gets through but proceeds to miss the cut, they then rack up more expenses for the week and lose more money. For example, players will have a minimum of four extra nights at a hotel and caddie expenses. It's possibile a player can end up losing more money for getting through a Monday qualifier.

I will give another example of how the PGA Tour lacks price control when it comes to their qualifiers. When I turned pro in 2013,

---

[20] TJ Vogel succeeded in qualifying eight times during the 2018 season —the most Monday qualifiers in a year.

the reorganization of the Tour had already happened and the price of Web.com qualifiers was $450 for six spots at two locations (for a total of twelve). However, the previous year, the price was $350 for seven spots at two locations (fourteen in total). So not only were the entry fees cheaper, there was also an extra qualifying spot. Again this goes back to the issue that the PGA Tour has a monopoly on professional golf and they can charge whatever price they want. Golfers will be forced to pay if they want a chance to qualify for tournaments. I have heard the argument that the PGA Tour sets their qualifying prices high because they want to discourage people who have no chance of qualifying. However, that is complete nonsense. I have seen scores in Web. com Monday qualifiers in the 90s. People will play in the qualifiers just for fun because the $450 is meaningless to them. The people who are really affected by the high entry fees are the golfers who are talented but cannot afford to pay the price.

I have heard golfers complain about the entry fees for Q-School and Monday qualifiers. While I do agree with them that the PGA Tour's prices are high, nobody is forcing them to play in them. If a golfer has such an issue with it, quit golf and do something else with life. But the reality is that if a golfer wants to progress their career they must play in these qualifiers, and without financial backing, it is impossible to truly pursue a career in golf.

I have often fantasized about the only way the PGA Tour would lower their entry fees. I will start off by saying the possibility of this happening is less than zero percent and completely absurd, but I will indulge you with the way it could be done. The only way to make the PGA Tour lower their prices would be to have all golfers start boycotting Monday qualifiers and Q-Schools in an effort to create some sort of bargaining power. However, the inherent issue is that if by some miracle a successful boycott was organized, there would always be a few golfers who would ruin the plan by signing up for the qualifier. For example, if six or less people signed up for the qualifier per site they would get into the tournament simply by completing a round of golf. It wouldn't matter what they shot. And why wouldn't they? I mean, if I found out that I could get into a Web.com event simply by signing up for a Monday qualifier, why wouldn't I? I wouldn't care about anybody's boycott. I would want the opportunity to play in the Web.com event. That is why this plan needs to go one step further—and this is where it gets even more ridiculous. The golfers organizing the boycott would have to hire Tony Soprano or some mafioso to stand on the first tee. If a golfer dared to play golf that day, the thug would literally break their thumbs so that they couldn't play a round and turn in a scorecard. Unfortunately, there is not a reasonable solution to controlling the cost of qualifiers, so the PGA Tour will continue to rip golfers off.

Another issue I have with the Tour has to do with sponsor exemptions. Now one of the most ridiculous things about golf is that for certain tours golfers can buy a spot in some tournaments. I am not sure of the exact rules, but I definitely know that for some Web.com events if an organization or individual pays enough money (at least $10,000), they have the right to give someone a spot in the tournament. For instance, this guy Julio Bell, who was a successful businessman in Colombia, more than likely bought a spot into the 2018 Colombia Championship. His competitive golf experience included playing on the Golf Channel Am Tour where his best score was an 87. Not surprisingly he proceeded to shoot a stellar 93-105 in the Web.com event. However, I also know other very capable golfers who have either bought their way into tournaments or used their connections to get spots into tournaments. Now to me this is a joke. Does this sound like the way professional sports should be conducted? It should be totally based on merit and playing ability. It is so wrong to allow someone to buy their way into a tournament. It is un-American in my opinion. By allowing someone to purchase their way into a tournament, they are taking a spot away from someone who is more deserving of it. For example, someone who has conditional status on the Web.com Tour. The person with conditional status could have used that tournament to earn prize money and potentially improve their status. Unfortunately, the Tour decides to allow sponsors to give exemptions to undeserving golfers just because they have financial backing or some connection. Truly and utterly disappointing.

Along these lines, the Web.com Tour and PGA Tour has given exemptions to undeserving athletes and celebrities in order to try to boost ratings and crowds. An example of this is when these tours gave exemptions to Jerry Rice, John Smoltz, Jake Owen, Tony Romo, and Steph Curry.

John Smoltz was given one sponsor exemption into the 2011 South Georgia Classic. He shot a solid 84-87 to miss the cut by twenty-seven shots and finish in last. Steph Curry shot 74-74 in the 2017 Ellie Mae Classic to finish in 148th place, and in the same event in 2018, he shot 71-86 to finish last. Tony Romo was given exemptions to the PGA Tour event in the Dominican Republic where he shot 77-82 to finish last in 2018, and 79-80 in 2019 to miss the cut by seventeen shots. He was also given an exemption into the 2019 Byron Nelson classic where he shot 76-74 to finish in 148th place. Another debacle was when country singer Jake Owen was given a sponsor exemption into the 2018 Nashville Golf Open, shot 86-86, finished last, and narrowly missed the cut by thirty-one strokes.

Jerry Rice received four exemptions into Nationwide Tour[21] events. All because he was a celebrity who wanted to pursue a "professional golf career." In Jerry Rice's first Nationwide Tour event, the 2010 Fresh Express Classic, he shot a stellar 83-76 to finish one shot ahead of last. Then in his second event, the 2010 BMW Charity Pro-Am, Jerry fired a solid 92 in the first round. In the second round, his caddie proceeded to use a rangefinder during the tournament which led to a DQ. In 2011, Rice played in the Fresh Express Classic, where he really grinded to shoot 81-82, and what place do you think he finished this time? Man, you are really good at guessing another last place finish! To wrap up Mr. Rice's career, he played in the 2012 TPC Stonebrae Championship, where he shot 86 in the first round and was seven over on the next nine before he decided to withdraw from the event. Some "pro golf career" Jerry had.

Amongst any other sport, golf is a game that is totally based on score and merit. There are no politics and the size of your wallet or celebrity status shouldn't allow people to play in events. Believe me, I don't care if a golfer plays bad if they deserve to be out there. Such as a player who got through Q-School, a Monday qualifier, or have some sort of conditional status. But it is downright disgraceful when undeserving people start taking spots away from deserving golfers who are trying to make a living. In one of those eleven events between John Smoltz, Jake Owen, Tony Romo, Steph Curry, and Jerry Rice, a golfer who earned the right to be in those events could have had a breakthrough week and maybe propelled their career. Instead, it was wasted on undeserving celebrities. Just ask Michael Arnaud and Nate Lashley how important

---

[21] What the Web.com Tour used be known as.

every spot in a field is. In the 2018 BMW Championship, Arnaud was the last player to make the field because somebody withdrew from the event and he took full advantage of the start by winning the event and securing his Web.com card for the 2018 and 2019 seasons. In a similar situation Lashley won the 2019 Rocket Mortgage Classic, solidifying his Tour card for at least two years. If one undeserving person was in either field, they would have never had those weeks. When these celebrities play in pro events, it's like allowing Tiger Woods to play in the NBA Developmental League for a few games and take playing time away from someone who is trying to make it to the NBA. I don't blame the celebrities for taking the exemptions—who wouldn't want to be given the opportunity to play in a Web.com or PGA Tour event? The issue is with the Tour that allows such nonsense to occur. It's wrong.

In terms of the PGA Tour, I can think of one specific instance when they gave an exemption to a capable golfer who was still undeserving of it. I am referring to Chase Koepka in the 2017 and 2019 New Orleans Zurich Classic. In this event, the PGA Tour switched up the format to be a two-man team event. The rules of how to get in the event were as follows: players with the higher priority ranking were able to choose their partner given they had PGA Tour status and some sponsor exemptions were given out. As Chase didn't have PGA Tour status, he was admitted into the field on a sponsor exemption. The reason I have an issue with Chase receiving a sponsor exemption is that he didn't deserve to be in that field because he didn't have any PGA Tour status. Now I am not taking anything away from Chase. He is a great golfer, he was an All-American at the University of South Florida and a member of the Challenge Tour[22] before he received the exemption in 2017. That is

---

[22] The Challenge Tour is the second-tier golf tour in Europe. It's basically the equivalent of the Web.com Tour in Europe.

nothing to sneeze at. However, there are a lot of golfers who had similar resumes and didn't play in the event. What's the difference? If I had to guess the only reason Chase played is because Brooks is his brother. Now I have no idea how the PGA Tour or Zurich decided who gets sponsor exemptions so I am going to have to speculate here, which I hate to do, but I must to prove my point. Brooks was a top twenty golfer in the world in 2017 and, in my opinion, can draw a crowd. He bombs the golf ball and I believe he pulls some weight with the sponsors of that tournament. I believe that Brooks has the leverage to say, "I want my brother to be my partner," and the sponsors will agree to his terms since Brooks has star power. By 2019, his star power was even bigger as a three-time major winner. Thus it is essentially nepotism. In addition, maybe Zurich liked the fact that there would be a team of brothers. I admit, it is neat. However, professional golf is not about what is neat, good feelings, good stories, or any of that. It is only about scoring and was that score good enough to qualify, win, etc. If the answer to that is "yes," then congratulations, well deserved. If the answer is "no," then the golfer needs to play better. No politics, no connections, and no nepotism! The fact that Brooks and Chase tied for fifth in 2017 doesn't justify the exemption.

Let me paint another picture to illustrate my point. Let's say that my best friend is Jordan Spieth. Now, Zurich obviously wants Spieth to play in their event because he is a star. But let's say that Jordan gave an ultimatum where he said, "I will only play in your event if you allow Jason Burstyn to be my partner." Zurich might say "yes" because they want Spieth at their event even though I have no right to be out there. What is worse is that this was a team event and I could of piggybacked off of Jordan to make a ton of money. Better yet, if we won I would have a two year exemption on the PGA

Tour. Imagine that I received an undeserved spot on Tour, depriving someone who has some status on the PGA Tour a spot. All of this would have happened because my best friend is Jordan Spieth and he essentially won the tournament for me. I know that there would be two days of alternate shot in the tournament where I would have had to play well. But on the best ball days, Jordan could have gone crazy and shot two rounds of 60 to essentially win the tournament on his own. Once again, some of these exemptions are just plain wrong.

To illustrate how important starts are on the Web.com and PGA Tour, I will tell you a story about my teammate when he qualified for the Puerto Rico Open. He was on the putting green the day before the first round and a player's caddie asked him how much it would cost "to get sick." He first offered him $5K, then $10K, but my teammate turned it down. The reason he was trying to bribe my former teammate was that this golfer was one of the first alternates and wanted to get into the event. This goes to show how important starts are on these tours, that players are willing to bribe other players to not play in events just so they have the opportunity to improve their status—another reason the Tour should never give spots to undeserving golfers.

I have heard the argument that sponsors put up a large portion of the prize money for tournaments so they have the right to give exemptions to whomever they want. I do live on planet earth and realize that money makes the world go round and without a sponsor's money there might not be a golf tournament. In addition, I totally understand why a sponsor would want Steph Curry to play in their event. It gives the company a lot of publicity and exposure. I mean, who in America has heard of the company Ellie Mae? Probably a vast majority of America's population has not. However, when Ellie

Mae has Steph Curry play in their event I'm sure a lot of people started to Google "what is Ellie Mae?" or "what does Ellie Mae do?" So I get it from a company's perspective. However, this is where the Tour needs to step in and set up strict guidelines or qualifications for who is allowed to receive sponsor exemptions. These qualifications should be very rigid and based on high playing ability. Here are some hypothetical guidelines that the Tour can impose on sponsors for their exemptions: "Company XYZ can only give a sponsor exemption to someone with the following golfing credentials: the Division I collegiate player who won the NCAA championship, the top rated DII collegiate golfer in the nation, a golfer who finished fiftieth to seventy-fifth in final stage of Q-School, or the golfer who wins the Florida Open." Those rules are very specific and measurable. In addition, if a sponsor wants to sell a spot there is a right way to do that as well. For example, I know that the Web.com Tour has sold spots to certain Hooter's Tour events. Then, whichever golfer wins the event, the player earns a spot into the sponsors Web.com event. While these situations might not be as glamorous as having Jerry Rice play in the event, they are the right way to give out sponsor exemptions. The Tour should have more honor and eliminate exemptions based on nepotism, money, or celebrity status.

In conclusion, I hope that I have painted a pretty good picture of the life of a pro golfer and how difficult it is to make it on Tour. The likelihood of a golfer making it on Tour is very small. A golfer has to be absolutely phenomenal at golf. Shooting even par will lead you to the poor house in a hurry. I would like to make a finance analogy as to how risky it is to pursue a career in golf. If the average DI collegiate golfer decided to pursue a career in golf I believe it's similar to investing in the most speculative penny stock. That golfer or any investor who were to financially back a mini tour golfer with no status on any tour is just about guaranteed to lose all of their money. The chances of receiving a return on their investment is very small unless this golfer is an absolute world beater.

Because a professional golf career is so risky I believe that kids who have dedicated their lives to golf should try to broaden their horizons and see what other opportunities there are in the world besides golf. To use myself as an example, I started playing golf when I was ten years old and continued throughout high school. I never had any small part-time summer jobs, such as working in grocery stores or at summer camps, as I was always traveling and playing in golf tournaments. I don't really have regrets about that, but when I entered college, I noticed that my friends who didn't play sports were getting various internships over the summer. They were getting valuable work experience and I started to wonder if I should try to do something similar. I was twenty-one years old and didn't even have a resume. While in college, I continued to play in golf tournaments over the summer. I remember after my fourth year of school (my redshirt junior year), I became eager to get some work experience outside of golf and an opportunity arose to do a two-month paid internship at a bank in Denver. I discussed it with my parents a lot, saying, "Shouldn't I get some work experience—something outside of golf to broaden my horizons and see if I like working in an office?" My mom was very encouraging, saying things like, "Yes, why not try something different, get some work experience." My dad, on the other hand, was not as encouraging. Although he never outright said "don't get that internship" and maintained that I could do whatever I wanted, he kind of gave me backhanded encouragement. He would say things like, "After next year, aren't you going to turn professional?

If so, why are you going to waste two months not playing golf if that's what you're going to do after graduation?" He would also say, "If you are trying to get a job then you are not totally focused on making it as a golfer." Although I somewhat agree with that, getting some work experience would not have been the worst thing in the world. Perhaps it would have helped mitigate my fear of not making it in golf because I would have had some other experience to fall back on—though this issue compared to my other mental garbage was less than peanuts. I don't want to give an unfair portrayal of my father. He is a very loving and supportive person, and was simply giving his advice on the matter at hand. I absolutely had the choice to take that job. I didn't have to listen to my dad, but was very influenced by what he told me and, ultimately, I didn't take it. I sometimes have regrets about not taking that internship even though I played some of the best golf of my life that summer. If I had taken it I believe one of two things would have happened: 1) I would have realized that I absolutely despised working in an office and I would have worked extra hard to get better at golf knowing that if I didn't get better, I'd be working in an office; 2) I wouldn't have minded or enjoyed working in an office and would have realized that there are other things in the world besides golf. In addition, taking two months off of golf wouldn't have really affected my game—your skills aren't going to deteriorate so fast if you're skilled enough to play college golf. I would have still been able to practice on the weekends.

In my opinion, if a college golf coach has their players' best interest in mind, they should strongly encourage their players to seek work experience outside of golf for one summer. Then I believe one of the two realizations I stated above will occur. The player will realize they hate whatever other type of work so much and will work that much harder at golf or they will realize they enjoy other things. If they realize they enjoy other matters, golf could become more relaxing and they may end up playing better as a result of not caring as much about golf. However, this will probably not happen. College golf coaches' jobs depend on the performance of their players so why would they want them doing anything besides practicing and playing, even though I just made an argument that it could possibly help a golfer's game. I would like to say that I did talk about this job opportunity with my college coach and he thought it would be a good experience and was very supportive of the idea.

The opportunity cost with golf is tremendous. Kids give up a lot. By taking an untraditional path, golfers risk falling behind the eight-ball in terms of work experience if they don't want a career in golf, whether that be playing or working at a golf course. To be fair it's not as if golf is the only activity out there that has an opportunity cost associated with it. Everything in life is an opportunity cost. For example, I once talked with one of my professors whose kids were very dedicated to chess. He told me how he was worried that his kids' studies would suffer because they spent so much time playing chess. I told him that I thought there is an opportunity cost when a person is very dedicated to something. I enjoy golf and I liked what I did growing up, I just wish I understood the way the world worked better at a younger age in terms of jobs, money, and things outside of golf. I didn't start asking myself these questions until I was about twenty-one. I feel I was not given all the information I should have been. I didn't realize the opportunity cost that was occurring by not exploring other options outside of golf. Had I known what was occurring I would have done things a lot differently.

CHAPTER 6

The Interviews

Now that I have expressed my opinions and views of golf psychology I hope that you can tell I had bad experiences with the industry and would never recommend it to anyone. However, I am only one person with my opinion(s). That's why I am now going to share various interviews I did with professional golfers who made it to a very high level. This chapter, in my opinion, is the most important in the book as it shows how successful golfers have thought differently, yet were successful. I would have never written this book if I didn't get the following interviews.[23] I think it's important to hear what successful golfers have to say because they are the ones who achieved success at this game. I want to be clear that just because they say something or make a claim, doesn't make it true or that it will work for everyone—it's their personal approach to different parts of the game and what has worked for them.

The questions I ask have to do with the issues I struggled with. I was curious to see if golfers at the top had similar issues to me. I asked the same questions to each interviewee for the most part, to help illustrate how they will have different answers to similar questions. They have no idea who I interviewed or what the other golfers said to the

---

[23] Interviews were conducted in 2016.

same questions. They have their own opinions on the questions I ask. There may be some overlap in theories, but overall their experiences and processes are unique. I truly hope that when you're through with reading these interviews that you're convinced of my belief that **there is no right or wrong** way to think in golf.

ERIK COMPTON

CAREER HIGHLIGHTS

- Highest World Golf Ranking: 71
- 2001 Walker Cup member
- Roughly $4.5 million in career earnings
- 2004 Canadian Tour Order of Merit Winner
- 2005 Hassan II Golf Trophy champion
- One Web.com Tour Victory
- Second place 2014 US Open
- Five top 10s on PGA Tour

I wanted to interview Erik because I have known him for a long time. I am not particularly close to him or anything like that, but we do know each other and went to the same high school. He is about ten years my senior. My favorite thing about Erik is his confidence; in my mind he always looks cool and collected like nothing can rattle him. Another reason I like him is that he once gave me a motivational talk when I was hitting golf balls on the range (I think my dad may have asked him to talk to me). He said something along these lines: "Jason, you're a nice guy and all, but you just seem soft to me. If Ricky Fowler was hitting golf balls and he saw me (Erik Compton) he would be saying I am going to kick that old guy's ass. You need to become more that way." I always like it when people give it to me straight.

INTERVIEW QUESTIONS

Have you ever seen a sports psychologist or shrink for golf? If yes, what did you talk about or work on?

I worked with a sports psychologist once or twice. But I didn't really get into it because I drew strength from my personal life with people I was surrounded by. I see my swing coach as a sports psychologist in a way. I once saw Jack Nicklaus hitting bunker shots and working with somebody at Murfield and got really turned off by the profession. I felt that the psychologist who was with Jack wasn't really helping him and didn't have Jack's best interest in mind. He was more there for his own benefit. I don't think there is a sports psychologist who is going to hypnotize you into becoming a better golfer.

What motivated you to get the point where you are at? To be the best? Money? Something else?

To be the best. I have always been wired that way since I was a kid. I just wanted to be the best at any athletic movement.

What was your economic status growing up?

| Upper middle class. No country clubs growing up.

Which parent encouraged or pushed you with golf? What did this parent/parents instill in you?

| Mostly my dad. He was not necessarily hard on me all the time but he also had no problem telling me what I needed to improve on if something needed to get better. He was very concerned if I ever thought of quitting. There was a time where I thought about becoming a normal teenager and moving to Norway and forgetting about golf.

I then told Erik about my concern of not making it as a professional golfer and how I would be in a hole in terms of work experience. He explained how he never had that issue because he always felt his parents were behind him. I still had that issue even though I had my parents' support.

When warming up on the range before a round what are your thoughts? For example: "I'm gonna tear these people apart;" "I'm gonna set the course record today;" "I'm never going back to the mini tours." Something completely different?

| I don't really necessarily get into a certain mindset. I'm more in tune with my body and figuring out how I am going to get prepared for the long day. I see what shots I am going to play and what I am going to take to the course. I'm just trying to do my job. I don't concern myself with what others are doing. It is irrelevant what others are doing. I lean

on my preparation, resting up, drinking water, and getting hydrated. Early in my career I did not know how to act. Now I know who I am, I am comfortable with who I am, and you just need to play to your personality. There is no right or wrong answer to what gets you going. I've been around Tiger and it seemed like he was in the zone or that's what people would say when they saw him. But in my mind he probably just wanted to avoid people without getting bothered. Everybody wants a piece of your energy when you get to that level. I've avoided situations because I knew that it was going to distract me from getting rest, conserving energy, or something along those lines.

Were you ever intimidated by an opponent or did any opponents ever make you feel uncomfortable?

The only person I have ever felt uncomfortable around was Tiger Woods in 2001. As I have gotten older, I almost seek that feeling of being uncomfortable because it makes me feel alive, even if it is for no reason at all. I can remember when I was playing in PGA Tour events when I was eighteen and I thought I was going to lose my knees because I was so nervous. For example, I am going to Hawaii to start the 2016 season and I have not been able to practice that much, but practicing is not what makes a good pro. Being able to handle everything that is thrown at you in a tournament is what makes a good pro.

Do you think people can train themselves to handle pressure better?

There are some golfers who just have the ability to handle a lot of pressure at a young age, such as a Jordan Spieth or Tiger Woods. I feel that I have been able to handle pressure much better the older

I have gotten. Being endowed with the ability to handle pressure is a gift just as much as athleticism. Some people are much more athletic than me but they do not have a mind like I do. In my opinion, it's better to have a great mind and not be that athletic. Even though people have certain personalities, it is tough to change your mind or mental habits because it is almost more of a pattern more than anything. You have to be able to break the bad patterns to change. I have hung around Chi Chi Rodriguez and he used to say winning is a habit just as much as losing is a habit. It is tough to change that. I have been around a lot of high profile athletes, such as Alex Rodriguez, and he really believes that he is the greatest thing on earth. I tell my caddie that I am the greatest all of the time. If you are not able to say that to yourself and feel comfortable with that, then you will not be good at anything. When I was on the Canadian Tour and I won an event I said that I am one of the best players in the world. What I meant by that was that I am good enough to play on the PGA Tour.

What's your take on Patrick Reed's comments after winning the WGC?

In the end nobody really cares. In this game you kind of just rent time. It's not that significant in the end, it is just a means to an end. Everybody has their moment in the sun. When Patrick Reed said his comments he wanted to flex and have his moment. I do not feel the need to do that on the PGA Tour. I am just here to make my money, and in my mind, nobody really cares so there is no need to say comments like that. I feel that the game has a funny way of coming after you for saying things like that. Like Karma. I feel that it is ridiculous to flex on the PGA Tour because everybody is great and on any given week somebody can have a great week.

When did you know you were good enough to make it?

When I was seventeen or eighteen. I played in some PGA Tour events and saw how the game was being played and I knew I could make money playing this game.

Do you have intrusive or negative thoughts? Or is your mind constantly positive and full of confidence? Or, even better, is your mind able to go blank?

No, not really. I do get down on myself from time to time. When I take time away from golf is where I gain my confidence. I don't see how hitting balls over and over is going to make me better. I gain my confidence from fishing, fly casting, doing other activities, resting, clearing my mind, or reminiscing with my friends. Doing those activities helps me put the game in perspective. Another thing that gives me confidence is what I have gone through in my life and knowing that others would not have been able to get where I have if they had those issues.[24]

On a scale of 1-10, with 10 being the highest, how confident would you say you are on the golf course?

I am probably around an 8.

---

[24] Erik is a two-time heart transplant recipient.

Do you love to show off how good you are?

I used to enjoy it more when I was younger, but now it is a different thing. It is more of self-satisfaction. I do not feel judged by other people. I only feel judged by the game. When you play the game long enough there are times when I feel the game is beating me up. You tend to focus only on the negatives.

What do you think of sports psychology as a whole? Do you think it is legitimate or BS?

As a whole, I think it is legitimate.

Do you think about your score when on the golf course? Do you look at the scoreboards?

Sometimes I do. I have a good feel for what is going on the course and I do not necessarily feel the need to look that often. But I will look if I need to.

Do you get nervous during tournaments or practice for what seems like no reason at all?

No. There has to be a reason to get nervous, such as to make the cut on the sixteenth hole or something. There must be a legitimate reason.

Are there any people that you felt like it was harder to play in front of, such as someone you knew in the crowd?

No.

What do you think it takes to make it as a professional golfer?

A lot of belief, a lot of hard work, takes a lot of athleticism, takes discipline, and knowing how to win at different levels.

Feel free to add any comments or thoughts about anything golf-related or not.

A lot of golf is just about believing in yourself. If you don't believe you are great, then nobody else will.

POSITIVE TAKEAWAYS

▶ I like that Erik is not obsessed with sports psychology and how he sees his swing coach as "psychologist in a way." Along the same lines I heard how Jimmy Walker talked to Bruce Bowen, the basketball player, for advice on his mental game. You don't need to be a mental guru and/or have a degree in psychology to help someone with their issues. And just because someone has those qualifications doesn't necessarily mean that they will give good advice.

▶ I thought it was interesting when he talked about Tiger and how people perceive him as being in the zone when perhaps all he wanted was to get from point A to point B. It goes to show that nobody knows what's going on in a person's mind and it's absurd when commentators try to guess what a golfer is thinking—they have no clue. At the same time, it's not like Erik has a clue either, but I found it interesting. It also reminded me of a pretty funny interview where a reporter asked Bob Knight something about a "game face." He responded, "What is a game face?" and proceeded to make various ridiculous-looking faces. It's just cliché nonsense.

▶ I found his comment that certain people are endowed with a better ability to handle pressure than others interesting, and agree that it's very tough to change mentally because it is more about breaking habits. The person needs to make a lifestyle change. You can't just make a new year's resolution and then "poof" you are mentally fixed.

▶ I loved how he said he got confidence from doing things outside of golf because it goes against a major cliché of "the hardest worker will win." Erik enjoys fishing and other activities. That's what works for him, so good for him. Golfers don't necessarily need to be like Vijay Singh and hit balls until their hands bleed.

▶ I would like to end with my biggest take away from the interview, which is what Erik told his caddie: "I am the greatest all the time. And if you are not able to say that to yourself you will not be great at anything." Yes, people need to be trained and need to be competent or else saying something like that is meaningless and has no substance. But once you have obtained a certain level of expertise, you should feel as confident as possible—this can be said about any profession, such as running a hedge fund, being an engineer, a financial analyst, a chef, or whatever. You need to believe in yourself because, as Erik said, no one is going to do it for you.

NEGATIVE TAKEAWAYS

Now before you all think I am solely going to agree with everything my interviewees have to say, I will also tell you what I disagree with from each interview.

▶ It seemed in Erik's mind that there was no need for Patrick Reed's comments, as he said, "The game has a way of getting back at you." I will always like what Reed said as he gave an unfiltered answer and wasn't being cliché. What's wrong with saying "I feel like I am a top five player in the world?" Especially when you are ranked somewhere in the top twenty. Who cares if Reed wanted to talk some trash? He won the tournament and was excited, so good for him.

GONZALO FERNANDEZ-CASTANO

CAREER HIGHLIGHTS

- Highest world ranking: 27
- Roughly €9 million on European Tour
- Roughly $2.1 million on PGA Tour
- Seven European Tour Victories
- Four top 10s on PGA Tour

INTERVIEW QUESTIONS

Have you ever seen a sports psychologist or shrink for golf? If yes, what did you talk about or work on?

When I was playing my best I never needed a sports psychologist. I could basically do it myself, there was a lot of confidence. In the last couple of years, things have not been as good. About a year ago I started working with a sports psychologist and it has been great. What we are talking about and working on is how I talk to myself on and off the golf course inside my head. It got to a point where it was very negative. It was not good at all. The person I have been working with is a school teacher in America, but used to be a psychologist in Spain.

What motivated you to get to the point where you are at? To be the best? Money? Something else?

I came over to America from Europe because I wanted to compete against the best. While I was comfortable playing on the European Tour, the money is way better on the PGA Tour. But it had more to do with the competition—the best players in the world are here, and I wanted to test myself against the best.

What motivated you growing up?

I played a lot of sports growing up, but golf captivated me. It was the fact that you are playing against yourself, the golf course, and trying to improve every time you go out there. I used to play tennis, soccer, and basketball. In those sports you're always playing against somebody else. With golf, it's against yourself, and that's what attracted me.

Do you love to show off how good you are at golf? For example, if somebody was watching you practice would you feel like it was an opportunity to show off your ability?

I think I am the other way around. My self-esteem is kind of low compared to some of the other guys I know. I have seen the best of the best and I know my limitations.

I wanted to dig further into this question so I asked: Would you like a crowd to watch you if you were practicing at a local golf course in Miami?

I don't mind a crowd. Being a professional athlete, I got used to it and I don't mind it. When I do practice, I like to be more on my own. I don't like to play games or other things with other players. I like to do my own thing and I am not trying to show off or anything.

What was your economic status growing up?

My family was well off so, thank God, I did not have to worry about that. My parents were able to take me back and forth from the golf course especially during the week. Money was not an issue at home and that always helps.

Did you ever get uncomfortable when you were doing really well, like -5 in a round?

Yes, I do—but I like that feeling. When you get that feeling, it means something to you. I like being on the first tee and getting those butterflies—I feel that helps me play my best. I am not able to shoot 59 like some of these people like nothing happened. When I am doing well, it feels like my swing does not flow as well as it did in the beginning of the round.

Do you like to jaw on the golf course, kind of joke around, or talk trash? Do you know any players who do?

When I play with my friends I do, but never in a tournament. I would never do that to my fellow players on Tour or during competition.

I asked Gonzalo if he knew anyone who did, and while he didn't give names, he said during practice rounds, on the driving range, and off the course people do, but it's all business once on the course.

Which parent encouraged or pushed you with golf? What did this parent/parents instill in you?

My dad was the one who played golf and took me around. He always pushed hard work on me. Talent is, of course, important; but if you really want to succeed, hard work gets you there. In the old days, talent may have been enough, but nowadays you need more than that. You see how hard these guys work, like Tiger and

Rory. If they are working hard and they are as talented as they are, you probably need to work as hard as them, if not harder.

How would you describe your mindset for your career? For example: "I'm gonna crush everyone today;" "I'm gonna set the course record today;" "I'm never going back to the mini tours." Or something completely different?

My mindset has always been one step at a time. First I focus on making the cut, starting the tournament well, and moving up the leaderboard. If I was close to the lead on Sunday, my mindset was I would really start to enjoy myself and play my best because I would really start to focus one shot at time and that always worked pretty well for me. I remember the first time I was in contention in a European Tour event to win and I ended up winning it. I was really surprised since I was so nervous on every shot on the back nine but I was so focused at the same time. You can't win a tournament on a Thursday, but you can certainly lose it. So you have to go slowly, and my goal is to make it to the weekend and advance on the field.

Were you ever intimidated by an opponent or did any opponents ever make you feel uncomfortable?

I felt it playing with Tiger. He's probably the most intimidating player I have ever played with. I also felt intimidated when I played with Seve. The first time I played with Tiger was in the Match Play around 2012 and there are so many things that go on around him. There are a ton of people, TV guys and media. I started birdie birdie and I was 2-up after two holes, but I lost the match. It's funny, when I feel the pressure I focus more on my procedure, my routine, on what I have to do, and the result is usually better. I think with me the harder the shot the better I do. Sometimes when it's a really easy shot, such as to a big fairway, I occasionally end up missing the fairway and I wonder how that was even possible.

When did you know you were good enough to make it?

When I was in my second-to-last year of college, I knew I was going to have a decent career as a golfer. I played in a couple of European Tour events as an amateur and I did pretty well. I was leading one event after a couple of days and I believe I was leading another one as well. That was when I realized it was worth it to give it a go. I was going to give it a chance for at least four to five years and see how it went. I have to say that I am glad that I did because I don't see myself anywhere else besides a golf course.

Did you ever feel judged or have any fears of judgement?

Yes, we are professionals and that comes with the territory. I have learned that it is impossible to please everybody. There is always going to be somebody that is not happy with a decision you make, but that is part of being an athlete. Someone is always going to evaluate what you did. To get over it, I said it's my life and I know what I have to do. I have to follow my own path. You can take advice from the people that matter to you, but, in the end, you have to make your own decisions. Like I said, you can't please everybody.

Are you superstitious at all?

| Not really. No lucky coins, no lucky tees, no lucky numbers.

Do you have intrusive thoughts or negative thoughts? Or is your mind constantly positive and full of confidence? Or, even better, is your mind able to go blank?

Yes, sometimes I know they are going to happen, such as thinking about results, the score, or what's going to happen the next few holes. That is what I call negative or intrusive thoughts. As soon as I get those thoughts it is important to identify them and change them for a positive or constructive thought. For me that is the most important, being able to identify them as soon as they happen and change them for good thoughts.

I wanted to understand this process more so I asked the following: If you were making the turn at -4 and started to think about the course record, would you consider that an intrusive thought? He said, "Yes that would be an intrusive thought." **So I asked what his process would be to redirect it in a positive way? He responded:**

To play golf you need to be very present minded. So the only way I know to do that is to focus on my breathing. I have done a bit of meditation in the past and I know the only way to be present is to have the body and mind connected. So that would be the first thing I do when I have one of those thoughts. Try to start forgetting about objectives and results because that takes you away from the present moment. Focusing on breathing has really helped me.

On a scale of 1-10, with 10 being the highest, how confident would you say you are on the golf course?

I think it really depends on the moment. Personally right now, my confidence is on the low side because my results have not been good lately. I know it shouldn't be like that and you should have confidence no matter what, but, in my case, it's not happening. I think personally my confidence depends on what is going on with my game. My goal would be to have the confidence you can see in some other players. Miguel Angel Jimenez would be a perfect example for me. He is self-confident in every aspect of his life—such as the way he walks—and he even believes he is good looking! For me, that is self-confidence. If you saw Rory Mcilroy and the way he walks on the golf course, you can see he is confident. Graeme McDowell would be another guy. The way he walks, the way he acts on the golf course, he's confident. That would be my goal. I'm probably on the other side of the spectrum, which is not good either.

What do you think of sports psychology as a whole? Do you think it is legitimate or BS?

Well, you know what, in the past I thought it was BS because I didn't need it. But then when things weren't going my way, I think it saved my career to be honest with you—because if I kept talking to myself the way I was a year ago my career probably would have been over. So I think it is important. If we had this conversation five years ago, I would have said it's bullshit.

Do you think about your score when on the golf course? Do you look at the scoreboards?

> I do like to have a goal of what I would like to score that day, but then once I tee off I kind of forget about it and start playing. But I do like to have a result in mind—of where I would like to go— before I tee off. I do keep an eye on scores to see how things are standing. It's like Tiger said: imagine playing a basketball game and having ten seconds to go and you don't know what the score is. So I do like to keep an eye on the leaderboards.

Do you get nervous during tournaments or practice for what seems like no reason at all?

> Yea, I do get nervous. I don't think that's something bad, having a little butterflies. But I like feeling a little nervous. Nervousness means it means something to you. It would be weird if I wasn't nervous. **When do you get nervous?** Starting off or it can be in the middle of the round—it depends. Sometimes it is in the middle of the round; it can be when you are leading a tournament on a Sunday, the first few holes, then it goes away, and it might come back. It's kind of weird. But normally on the first tee I am a little nervous, which I like. **Do you get nervous practicing?** No.

Are there any people that you felt like it was harder to play in front of, such as someone you knew in the crowd?

> No, not really. I wouldn't say so. I always enjoyed having people around—the more people the better. **Does it matter if you know**

the person or not? No, it doesn't matter. If Tiger Woods showed up to watch me play golf, I would probably get a little nervous, but I can't tell since it hasn't happened.

What do you think it takes to make it as a professional golfer?

Nowadays it takes to hit the ball a long way. You need to be a long hitter to make it as a professional. It takes a lot of commitment with the life of a tour pro, which isn't easy with all the traveling, being away from your family, and a lot of hard work. Talent is important, but it is not enough. Maybe in the old days it was, but now you have to put the hours in on the driving range, at the gym, and with a sports psychologist. It takes a lot of time but, of course, the reward is big if you succeed.

What do you think is the ideal mindset for a golfer?

Maybe I am not the one to answer this question. I think you have to ask these young guys. You see these young guys, such as Justin Thomas, Jordan Spieth—these twenty-two- and twenty-three-year-olds—and the way they behave on the golf course. It's just incredible. They look so experienced on the golf course. The perfect demeanor, if you ask me, is just try to enjoy yourself on the golf course, don't take it too serious. Take it serious, but not too serious.

POSITIVE TAKEAWAYS

▶ I liked how he said when he was playing his best he never needed sports psychology. It just goes to show that when

Gonzalo was winning all of these European Tour events he didn't need a "mental coach." In fact, he said that if I asked him five years ago if sports psychology was BS, he would have said YES. On the same note, I am happy that he felt that a psychologist helped him keep his career going.

▶ I could tell that Gonzalo wasn't fazed by crowds since he felt comfortable with them, whether the crowd consisted of people he knew or not, it didn't matter. Additionally, he said the more people the better. In my case, I didn't mind a crowd but didn't like performing in front of people I knew.

▶ I loved how Gonzalo talked about his goals during tournaments and how his first goal was to make the cut. All I ever hear from commentators is how the weekend rounds are the most important. But the reality is that if a golfer doesn't play pretty well the first two days, they are not going to have a chance to see the weekend. His quote—"You can't win a tournament on a Thursday, but you can certainly lose it"—sums up how important those days are.

▶ I like how Gonzalo watches leaderboards to see what's going on. This is in direct conflict with so many golf psychologists who maintain that golfers shouldn't look at the leaderboards because that means they are focused on results.

▶ Golf Psychologists often talk about how confidence cannot be dictated by your results or how you are playing. Gonzalo shows that that's not the way it works for everyone. I agree that it's best if you can boom with confidence all the time, but that's just not reality. As Gonzalo observed, his confidence at this current time is on the low side because he isn't getting the results he wants.

▶ My favorite take away from the interview was when Gonzalo discusses how he deals with being judged by others. I thought the following statement of his was very powerful: "You cannot make everybody happy. It's my life and I know what I have to do. I have to follow my own path. You can take advice from the people that matter to you, but in the end you have to make your own decisions." What I took from these remarks is that in a way you have be stubborn, know what works for you, and tell most people to go kick rocks.

NEGATIVE TAKEAWAYS

▶ I disagree with Gonzalo's comment that having butterflies means something is important to you. Gonzalo felt that but-terflies were helpful to him, but there is no reason you can't be calm and have something be meaningful for you. For most golfers, when they reach the middle of the round they lose their butterflies. So does that mean that those shots are no longer important to them? Of course not. Having nerves equate to meaningfulness is a fairly common school of thought in golf that I disagree with.

▶ I disagreed with some of his thoughts about what it takes to be a successful golfer. First, you don't have to spend time working on your mental game. I find it interesting that when he was playing his best on the European Tour, he didn't work with any psychologists. In addition, I do not think you have to spend hours in the gym be a great golfer. I can't say exactly what Gonzalo meant by this but I would like to comment that great golfers come in all shapes and sizes. Overweight ones: Tim Herron, John Daly, Craig Stadler, Angel Cabrera, Kiradech Apribarnrat, and many more. Average-statured ones: Pat Perez, Davis Love III, Fred Couples, and Rickie Fowler. Skinny ones: Justin Thomas, Sean O'Hair, Chesson Hadley, and Tiger as an amateur was skinny as a rail.

I thoroughly enjoyed talking to Gonzalo. He is an incredibly nice guy and was very honest—as you could tell by his answers.

STEVE JONES

CAREER HIGHLIGHTS

- Highest world ranking: 15
- Roughly $6.5 million in career earnings on PGA Tour
- Eight PGA Tour Victories, three runner-ups, 44 top 10s
- 1996 US Open Champion

INTERVIEW QUESTIONS

Have you ever seen a sports psychologist or shrink for golf? If yes, what did you talk about or work on?

I have not. My dad always said, "Do the best you can." If anybody was my coach it was him. He kept it simple. Just do the best you can and there is not much more you can do after that. You can't control anybody else's outcome.

What motivated you to get to the point where you are at? To be the best? Money? Something else?

I started playing golf when I was twelve. I loved golf. So, when I was twelve years old, I told my parents I wanted to be a pro golfer. I never really thought about the money, I just knew I wanted to play golf.

Do you love to show off how good you are at golf? For example, if somebody was watching you practice would you feel like it was an opportunity to show off your ability?

No. I practice so I can get better. I don't worry about what others think. Some people get wrapped into a lot of things—like how do my clothes look, am I too fat, too skinny? Or whatever it might be. You have to let those things go.

What was your economic status growing up?

There were eight people in my family. In the 1960s, we didn't have a lot in New Mexico. People would just play sports or sit in trees. Just do things outside. In the 1970s, my family moved to Colorado and that was the first time I started to swing a club. My father worked until the day he died and supported our family.

Did you ever get uncomfortable when you were doing really well, like -5 in a round?

Yea, definitely. I would get tight when I was playing well. I would get tight when I was playing bad. Some people handle it better than others. Golf takes a lot out of you. I would have moments when I was playing well and I would get tight. I would tell myself if this is what you want to do then embrace it and do it. Sometimes I handled it well, other times I did not.

Do you like to jaw on the golf course or kind of joke around? Do you know any players who do?

I joked around but never talked trash. I would maybe talk trash after doing something good. Golf humbles everybody. You could win a golf tournament then miss a cut the next week. It keeps you humble.

Which parent encouraged or pushed you with golf? What did this parent/parents instill in you?

No one pushed me. My parents were both talented. My mom was a good golfer. Whatever I wanted to do, my parents supported me. When I was twelve years old and told them I wanted to be a professional golfer, they supported me.

How would you describe your mindset for your career? For example: "I'm gonna crush everyone today;" "I'm gonna set the

course record today;" "I'm never going back to the mini tours."
Or something completely different?

I was always a grinder. Nothing came easy for me. If I didn't practice for three or four days I felt rusty. My grip never felt that comfortable. It did at some points when I was playing well but I was always having to make little adjustments and trying to improve. In terms of practicing I always doubled the amount of short game I did to the range. So if I hit balls for one hour, I would putt and do other short game activities for two hours. I wasn't always a consistent ball striker. If I putted well I always had a chance to win. I was always a good putter, so that kept me on Tour.

Were you ever intimidated by an opponent or did any opponents ever make you feel uncomfortable?

Sure—if somebody hit it twenty to thirty yards past me. I was never top ten in length, but more in the range of eleventh to thirtieth. I was also injured for about a third of my career. When somebody was longer than me, it wasn't like I said I can't beat them. It was just like: how do they hit it so far? I just stuck to my game and I knew I would putt better than them, so that was the equalizer.

When did you know you were good enough to make it?

I knew I was good enough in terms of scoring my senior year of college golf. I won two tournaments that year and in the spring I never finished outside the top ten. Going into every tournament I would say to myself that this is Q-School and I have to finish top fifteen. So when I got to Q-School, I did not treat it as a big deal. I just looked at it as another tournament and got through—even with a broken thumb.

Did you ever feel judged or have any fears of judgement?

People are always judging all the time. I always knew that even if you had a pretty swing, it doesn't mean you are going to play good golf. You learn from your mistakes and you can learn from others, mistakes as well. That way you don't make them yourself. In golf you will always make mistakes so it's important to keep learning.

Are you superstitious at all?

I'm not. Never did a certain thing. I tried not to be. Sometimes it would try to creep on me, but I never was.

Do you have intrusive thoughts or negative thoughts? Or is your mind constantly positive and full of confidence? Or, even better, is your mind able to go blank?

For me, if I was hitting a shot where there was a hazard and started to think about the trouble, I would focus on the shot, such as I am trying to hit a draw or fade. You're going to hit bad shots but you just move on. There are probably two thousand golfers who have enough skill to be on Tour, but what I think separates golfers is how well they handle it when they make bogeys. Do they dwell on it or do they move on? I believe you really have to go through your routine. When I was playing basketball, my free throw routine was three dribbles, look, and shoot. Routine is everything. When you get familiar with and stick to it, things come easier.

On a scale of 1-10, with 10 being the highest, how confident would you say you are on the golf course?

When playing badly, I was around a 5 or 6. If I was playing well, I was around a 9 or 10. It's hard to have confidence when you are shooting 77. My confidence was, for the most part, dependent on how I was playing. If I knew what I was doing was right—believed in it, stuck to it—and good scores followed, I was going to be confident.

What do you think of sports psychology as a whole? Do you think it is legitimate or BS?

When that stuff started in the 1980s and 1990s, all the psychologists were doing was listening to Tour pros and writing down what they said about how they thought. So it essentially started with Tour pros. They would then intermingle it with their psychology background. I think people should use what they can use. Whatever floats your boat. **Steve then started to talk about Chip Beck and how he is the most positive person he has ever encountered.** If Chip hit a bad shot, he would say something along the lines, "Chip, you can't do that." **Essentially Steve was saying that positive thinking will not save you. It's not going to prevent you from hitting bad shots.**

Do you think about your score when on the golf course? Do you look at the scoreboards?

No, I did not look at scoreboards. When I won the US Open in 1996, I did not look the whole day. On the last hole I asked my brother where I stood. So I did not get too involved in that. During that week, I read Ben Hogan's autobiography and finished it on Wednesday, the day before the US Open. In the book he emphasized the most important shot is the next one. You can't worry about what's behind you.

Do you get nervous during tournaments or practice for what seems like no reason at all?

It depends, most of the time I was pretty loose. Maybe on the first tee or if I was in contention. You learn to deal with adrenaline and how your body reacts. For example, at Hilton Head in 1987, I had a one shot lead on the last hole and hit it out of bounds. At the 1988 AT&T Pebble Beach, I was in a similar situation and said to myself, "You screwed this up last year at Hilton Head, let's learn from it. This time don't stop your body and swing through it." I hit a great drive and won the tournament.

Are there any people that you felt like it was harder to play in front of, such as someone you knew in the crowd?

I enjoyed having my friends or my parents come out. I like to talk when I am on the golf course and interact with people, so I always welcomed that.

In your opinion what do you think it takes to make it as a professional golfer?

It takes a special kind of person on how to handle the shot after a bad one. Nicklaus never threw a hissy fit; he was always class. Tiger is probably the one who got the maddest, but to me it made him braver. You've really got to do what works for you.

In your opinion what do you think is the ideal mindset for a golfer?

I don't think there is one. There are too many emotions, too many feelings, and people are different. Different people will have different feelings in their fingertips or in their body. You can't say there is one remedy that is going to help everybody. You have to move on to the next shot no matter how good or bad. All the best concentrators are the best golfers. That doesn't mean you are going to grit your teeth and say I am going to concentrate now. It's about focusing on your routine and things like that.

Feel free to add any comments or thoughts about anything golf-related or not.

The golf ball has really changed the game. When I was playing and hitting Balata golf balls, if you were to hit a bucket of golf balls you would maybe hit four or five straight shots. Now when you see Tour pros hitting, every shot is just dead straight. In my era we did not really hit straight shots. It's a different game nowadays. We used to have to really work the ball, such as hitting draws, fades, knockdowns, and other things. You still have to have a short game. I would love to watch a PGA Tour event where everybody in the field had to play with a Balata golf ball and see how they do. It was a different skill back then. Now it's just hit it and bomb it. I'm not saying we should go back to the way it was—it's just different.

POSITIVE TAKEAWAYS

▶ I like how Steve kept it fairly simple, he didn't like to overcomplicate things. He never saw any reason to see a sports psychologist. His philosophy was to try your best and there's nothing you can really do besides that.

▶ It seems that Steve wasn't affected by what people thought, which is a very valuable asset as a pro golfer.

▶ Steve had a similar issue to me where he would randomly get tight or nervous whether playing poorly or well. I thought his statement about getting nervous—how he would tell himself that if this is what he chose to do, he should embrace it when he was playing well—was valid. But, as he said, he struggled to accept it. I think that this is a great illustration of how there are no magic pills or anything to cure mental blocks or issues: while

Steve had rationalized it perfectly, his mind had trouble accepting it.

▶ I really liked how confident Steve was in regards to his putting. He always felt he could beat people because he was a better putter than his competition. Although golf is becoming more of a power game, Steve said his putter kept him on Tour for many years.

▶ I absolutely loved his approach toward Q-School and how he didn't treat it as a big deal. He viewed it as another college tournament and made it through. It's similar to how people put more importance on certain events. Yes, the majors are the biggest—and some people call the Players Championship the "fifth major"—but every tournament is the same in my opinion. You have to hit fairways, greens, and make putts. The media makes it seem that the only tournaments that matter are the majors, but that's ridiculous. Would you rather have Shaun Micheel or Lee Westwood's career?[25]

▶ Just like Gonzalo, Steve's confidence was dependent on how he was playing. I liked how he said it's tough to be confident when you're shooting 77.

▶ For me, the most interesting answer from Steve was when he was talking about how when sports psychology started in the 1980s and 1990s, psychologists would interview Tour pros, record and catalog their answers, and then base their

---

[25] Shaun Micheel only won one PGA Tour event, which happened to be a major championship. Whereas Lee Westwood has never won a major, but has had a very long and profitable career including over twenty European Tour victories and PGA Tour wins.

theories on how successful golfers thought. This illustrates how the profession relies heavily on anecdotal evidence and not necessarily on robust experimentation.

▶ I loved how Steve said you can be as positive as you want but it's not going to save you from hitting bad shots. I also liked how Steve drew upon a negative experience from the 1987 Hilton Head to help ensure that he didn't make the same error in the 1988 AT&T Pebble Beach. Mr. O would have said that this is a big no-no since he was thinking of a negative scenario and it would hurt his performance. Steve thought of a negative experience to improve a future performance and no mental guru can tell him he was wrong.

▶ Steve hit the nail on the head with what the main theme of the book is when I asked him what he thought the ideal mindset for a golfer was. He said there is no one ideal mindset; there are many emotions and feelings because people are different. People have different feelings in their fingertips and bodies. You can't say there is one mindset or remedy that is going to help everybody. This was beautifully said and he is essentially saying **there is no right or wrong.**

NEGATIVE TAKEAWAYS

I really did not have any negative takeaways from the interview. I liked everything he had to say.

CHIP BECK

CAREER HIGHLIGHTS

- Highest world golf ranking: 8
- Roughly $6.2 million on PGA Tour
- Three-time Ryder Cup member
- Four PGA Tour Victories
- Eighteen runner-up finishes, 80 top 10 finishes
- Shot 59 in 1991 Las Vegas Invitational

INTERVIEW QUESTIONS

Have you ever seen a sports psychologist or shrink for golf? If yes, what did you talk about or work on?

In 1984, I saw my first sports psychologist. He was from Ohio State and had success with football kickers. His main thing was if you can feel the shot, you can do the shot. After seeing him that week I played very well. I played with Jack Nicklaus in the final round that week and missed a playoff by one shot. That was my first experience with psychology and it had a powerful effect.

What motivated you to get the point where you are at? To be the best? Money? Something else?

I was just trying to be the very best at what I did. I wanted to play in big tournaments and play well. In the beginning, I played for trophies and for the love of the game. I feel that people who play for the money don't seem to make it as far as they could have and somewhat shorted their careers. Although Raymond Floyd was a big time gambler, and he obviously had a great career. I played for wins and played to hit great shots. Money is just a byproduct and will take care of itself.

Do you love to show off how good you are at golf? For example, if somebody was watching you practice would you feel like it was an opportunity to show off your ability?

Every pro golfer likes to have people interested in what they are doing and to perform for these people. Some people worry that there are people watching. But performers like to perform and want a stage. The bigger the stage the better. I always thought it was nice to have people watch and be interested in what I am doing.

What was your economic status growing up?

My dad was a dentist in North Carolina. I had ten brothers and sisters. I was pretty middle class. On my high school golf team, five people got Division I scholarships. I had a lot of competitive matches growing up.

Did you ever get uncomfortable when you were doing really well, like -5 in a round?

Everybody gets tight at one point or another. You may screw up a few times when you are doing well but you learn how to not make those mistakes again. **Our conversation then turned to the time he shot 59.** When I shot 59, there was a player in the field who shot in the very low 60s that week, so I saw that it could be done. My biggest issue in my career was that I would get too careful toward the end of tournaments. That is another form of choking to me.

Chip then started to talk about different topics and said the following.

I always felt it was easier to play with house money, such as after making the cut. **He began discussing the Ryder Cup and said it's great to qualify but it's not like winning a Tour event.** Tournaments are individual efforts and that is more important to me. Don't get me wrong playing in the Ryder Cup was one of the highlights of my life, but majors were more important to me. It's not like I thought about the Ryder Cup during the season and was trying to figure out how to qualify for it.

Do you like to jaw on the golf course, kind of joke around, or talk trash? Do you know any players who do?

I always enjoyed encouraging people about their game. I felt that if the group encouraged each other it would sort of carry momentum. I have had players try to walk in on me when I am putting and try to mess with my game. If somebody is trying to mess with your game, you have to stand your ground and let them know that is not going to fly. One thing I admire about Bernhard Langer and Jack Nicklaus is that they often got accused of slow play but they didn't let it affect them. It takes a strong individual to not be affected.

Which parent encouraged or pushed you with golf? What did this parent/parents instill in you?

My mother and I started playing golf the same day. My mom was a good putter. She could really roll the ball. She just really enjoyed the game. She never really instilled anything specific but she was always having a good time and that stuck with me. My dad was very interested in our education. He would give us a word of a day and things of that nature. He was a bricklayer's son. My grandfather would often tell my father if you don't do better in school you will be a bricklayer just like your father. All of my brothers and sisters have college degrees.

How would you describe your mindset for your career? For example: "I'm gonna crush everybody today;" "I'm gonna set the course record today;" "I'm never going back to the mini tours." Or something completely different?

Every week I had a different mental goal. For example, one week my goal would be to be mentally strong. One week my goal might be to totally focus on being relaxed. Another week it might be to focus on trusting my stroke. One week it might be to have the resilience to make my par putts on every hole. One week it was to say something positive after every shot no matter what. Having these goals helped keep me at nest.

Were you ever intimidated by an opponent or did any opponents ever make you feel uncomfortable?

One instance where I was intimidated was when I was playing in the World Match Play. I was tight, jet-lagged, and it was cold out. I was playing against Seve and he was loose. He stuck it to one foot on the first hole. I just said to myself: how am I going to beat that today? I ended up losing 9&8 to him. Another time was the first time I played with Raymond Floyd at the US Open. The first four holes, I was choking so bad. On the fourth hole, I hooked my ball in the woods and Floyd put his arm around me and said, "Settle down and just follow my lead and I'll take you to the top cause I'm winning this tournament." He was my boyhood idol and I wanted to impress him so I was so nervous. In general though, I always wanted to play with the best players. I liked playing with good players.

When did you know you were good enough to make it?

You never know when you are good enough to make it. I won state tournaments in high school. I won the All-America tournament in college, which was the second biggest event behind NCAAs. You just keep pushing forward and trying make it. You don't know when it's going to happen and in this game you are never where you want to be.

Are you superstitious at all?

No, not at all. I have too much faith to be superstitious. I have an unwavering commitment in knowing God provides for us. I don't believe in superstitions. In my opinion, they hold you back. Superstitions are fleeting. If you have superstitions, they can change and you can drive yourself crazy with them.

Do you have intrusive thoughts or negative thoughts? Or is your mind constantly positive and full of confidence? Or, even better, is your mind able to go blank?

Nobody has good feelings all the time. I was talking to Hale at the Memorial one year and he told me, "I am hitting the ball as bad as I ever have." He then went on to win the golf tournament. Nobody is good all the time. I have seen Tom Watson so disgusted and upset with his game that he was miserable. We have cycles of low confidence, low competency, and I had to learn to be strong in spite of weakness. It is part of the beauty of the game. You just need to pick up the pieces and keep moving on.

On a scale of 1-10, with 10 being the highest, how confident would you say you are on the golf course?

I was always pretty confident that I would do well. I would say a 9 or 10. It wasn't always like that though. When I started out playing professionally I had so little confidence. I had a bad marriage and it hurt my game. When I got past those problems, I felt like 9-10. It's funny, when my first wife threw me out of the house, I won two tournaments in the next three months. I was working with a marriage counselor when that happened.

The counselor told me that I owe it to myself to leave my issues with my wife at home and play the best possible golf I could and it worked for me. Those problems can hold you back. It affects you emotionally. That's just the way life goes. You do the best you can and move on. A good marriage can really help a golfer. My second marriage was a blessing and I am so happy I met her.

Do you think about your score when on the golf course? Do you look at the scoreboards?

I liked to know where I stood. It helped me out a lot. After a while I didn't really react to birdies or bogeys. You just put your best foot forward no matter what you score. You can't get wound up on how you are doing. I have heard people say after starting off with a three-putt that they are going to have a bad week. That is just stupid. It could have been that you misjudged the putt and it just happened to be on the first hole.

Do you get nervous during tournaments or practice for what seems like no reason at all?

Sometimes I would get anxious, but there was usually a pretty good reason for it. I was not neurotic or anything.

Are there any people that you felt like it was harder to play in front of, such as someone you knew in the crowd?

I guess there are people who expect certain things out of you. I always felt that this helped me. I never had issues with people watching me. I'll tell you a story about a spectator who was once driving me crazy. One week there was a guy in the crowd who was yelling at me for a few holes, saying how I owe him 10 percent of my winnings because he gave me a tip. I mean this guy was really driving me crazy and not leaving me alone. I told my brother, who was caddying for me that week, that this guy is driving me nuts. So he went up to this guy and said, "You need to leave and not come back. If you come back you are going to have problems with me."

What do you think it takes to make it as a professional golfer?

There are overriding qualities. A dedication to the craft. There is no way around it. A commitment to getting it done. There can be nothing lackadaisical about it. You have to have a short game.

What do you think is the ideal mindset for a golfer?

The most important quality that a golfer needs to have is the belief that I am going to the top and nothing is going to hold me back.

POSITIVE TAKEAWAYS

► Chip had a positive experience with sports psychology. While it was different from my experience, I'm happy it worked for him.

▶ He showed me that he was human and vulnerable at times, which I appreciated. For example, how issues from his first marriage were bringing him down or how he was nervous to play with Raymond Floyd. Despite these vulnerabilities, he was very confident and believed in his abilities.

▶ I liked how he described himself as a showman, and the bigger the stage, the more he relished it. I didn't have that mindset and I believe it's important to have that as a professional golfer. There are always going to be people watching, so if you don't enjoy that, you have less of a chance of being successful.

NEGATIVE TAKEAWAYS

▶ I disagree with Chip's comment about how golfers who play for money shorted their careers. I don't know if he was speaking about certain individuals but he also stated how some golfers, such as Raymond Floyd, did and were successful. There is nothing wrong with pursuing a career for money.

Chip is a great guy. I talked to him for two and a half hours. It was very interesting to hear his stories about his playing days. He really liked to elaborate and I felt he didn't hold anything back. I feel like I could call him tomorrow, and if I needed to crash at his house, he'd let me. He was incredibly nice.

BRUCE FLEISHER

CAREER HIGHLIGHTS

- Highest world ranking: 134
- Roughly $1.7 million on PGA Tour
- Roughly $14.8 million on Champions Tour
- 1968 US Amateur Champion
- One PGA Tour Victory, four runner-up finishes, 25 top 10s
- Eighteen Champions Tour Victories
- Twenty-three runner-up finishes, 116 top 10s

INTERVIEW QUESTIONS

Have you ever seen a sports psychologist or shrink for golf? If yes, what did you talk about or work on?

When I was forty-eight, I started working with Bob Rotella. I spent a couple of days with him. Two things I got from him were routine—which keeps me in the present—and picking the smallest target possible. This allows you to be very narrow-minded in your ball flight. He kept me in the game in the sense that he gave me an outlet to discuss my golf. Rotella wanted to know what was going on with his clients. He wanted his students to keep a diary of their statistics so they could find out what their weaknesses were and strengthen them.

What motivated you to get the point where you are at? To be the best? Money? Something else?

I was a journeyman in the 1970s. I struggled at the very best. When my wife got very sick in 1980, it made me reevaluate some things with golf. In the 1980s, I was the pro at Westview in Miami and worked there for seven years. In my heart though I never gave up the thought that I would get out there. In 1989, I won the Club Pro Championship, which is the biggest club pro tournament in the country. That win gave me five exemptions into PGA Tour events and I was finishing middle of the pack beating half the field. I thought to myself: I haven't played in seven years and I'm beating half of the field. At the time I was working at Williams Island and I hated my boss, he didn't honor the contract and I quit. I was forty-two years old at the time and there was a gambler at the club who sponsored me. I started off on the Hogan Tour and worked my way up to the PGA Tour. I won the Bank of Boston event in a seven-hole playoff against Ian Baker Finch and that got me to play through my forties. By that point, I was looking toward the Senior Tour in all honesty. When I was working at Williams Island, I would look in the papers and see the name Tom Shaw—who I played with growing up and would beat. But he was making $500K and I was making $50K giving lessons. That's when I decided I was going to play through my forties.

Bruce then started to talk about why he felt he was more success-ful on the Senior Tour than other more accomplished players, such as Fuzzy Zoeller, Lanny Wadkins, Andy North, Curtis Strange, and Ben Crenshaw. Bruce won eighteen times on the

Senior Tour, and between the five players listed previously, they won four tournaments. According to Bruce, the reason was that he played golf throughout his forties on Tour whereas they retired in their early forties:

> I was able to play through my forties, so I truly felt that some of my success was due to timing, fate, and never giving up. In regards to the timing when I was fifty, Jack Nicklaus was sixty, Gary Player was sixty-five, Arnold Palmer was seventy, Lee Trevino and Ray Floyd were sixty. They were not going to beat me. Their time had passed. The money definitely motivated me, I wanted to be comfortable. It was all about money. I also wanted to be respected.

Do you love to show off how good you are at golf? For example, if somebody was watching you practice would you feel like it was an opportunity to show off your ability?

> I enjoy helping people and I enjoy people. When I would practice, I would usually have a crowd, I would talk to the crowd, I would joke with them, and I would try to teach them what I was doing. So I wouldn't say I was showing off, but I was very comfortable.

Bruce then spoke about watching himself play tournaments that were recorded, which I thought was very interesting. He told me how he asked Lee Trevino, Arnold Palmer, and Ray Floyd if they liked watching themselves play when they were winning and they all said "NO." They never watched themselves because they

would be their own worst critic and find something they didn't like in their golf swing. **Bruce said,** I never liked my golf swing so I never watched myself.

What was your economic status growing up?

> I never knew what rich or poor was. We had a roof over our head in Wilmington, North Carolina. I started caddying for my father when I was seven years old. Growing up, I was a good baseball player, but what really got me into golf was when I was twelve years old I won the Donald Ross Invitational at Pinehurst. I remember that feeling of winning and said to myself, "I am going to go after this."

Did you ever get uncomfortable when you were doing really well, like -5 in a round?

> I had the chance to break 60 once. I wasn't scared to go low but was more of a consistent player. I did not really make bogeys. When you are playing well not much gets in your way. You can't be swing conscious. I was never comfortable going into the last round when I was leading. A lot of thoughts would swirl around my head.

Do you like to jaw on the golf course, kind of joke around or talk trash? Do you know any players who do?

> No. I'll talk, but I will say good shot. I was courteous and kind.

Which parent encouraged or pushed you with golf? What did this parent/parents instill in you?

> My dad was a consulting engineer. He never got behind me. My dad thought it was a gamble, and he was right. In my day, a given week was going to cost $2,000 so in a way it is gambling. A few people helped me, but I was mostly self-driven. I won the Panama Open, Jamaican Open, Brazilian Open, and Colombian Open. Winning breeds winning.

How would you describe your mindset for your career? For example: "I'm gonna crush everybody today;" "I'm gonna set the course record today;" "I'm never going back to the mini tours." Something completely different?

> I had different goals. I just wanted to survive and be respected. My wife was my biggest supporter, but she still wanted me home at 5 p.m. Other golfers were beating balls until it was dark out. I was not driven to be the best, I just wanted to make a living. That's why I feel achieving success at the age I did was far more satisfying. As opposed to some of these golfers who are given $50 million contracts at twenty-five years old. I believe they have no incentive. It is way too much money too early in their career. Where is the motivation? Where do they go from there? Being successful in my fifties was so rewarding.

Were you ever intimidated by an opponent or did any opponents ever make you feel uncomfortable?

Jack was probably the most intimidating guy. Faldo was also intimidating. He barely said anything—you would be lucky to get a greeting out of him. He just plotted along and played his round. I thought he was miserable out there but what a great player he was. If you hit a good shot, you would not hear anything from him. Let's just say that I enjoy him more in the booth than on the course.

Bruce then got into talking about people he did not like, which I enjoyed.

I did not like playing with Steve Elkington. J.C. Snead used to stand in your line and play games with you to try to mess with you.

I asked Bruce what Steve Elkington did to him to piss him off and he said the following:

I had been off the Tour for a while when I was working. I got into Augusta for winning a tournament that year and we were both fighting for a top twenty-four spot because that would have gotten us an exemption into the Masters the following year. I was beating him badly that day and he had not spoken to me all day. Late in the round he comes up to me and says, "Can I speak to you mate? Your caddie stepped in my line three times today, can you tell him to be more careful?" And I say to myself are you kidding me? If your caddie stepped in my line one time you would have heard about it. I bogeyed the last hole to finish twenty-fifth. I thought that was the worst gamesmanship ever played on me. I was too naive back then to totally understand that he was trying to rattle me. Overall I was disappointed in the way he conducted himself in order to try to get an edge on me.

182

When did you know you were good enough to make it?

I was always a good qualifier when it came to events such as Q-School. I never doubted myself or my ability.

Did you ever feel judged or have any fears of judgement?

At the end of the day no one is paying my bills. It is all about yourself in the end. The pressure we put on ourselves is strictly put on by us. The sun is going to come up tomorrow whether we play good, bad, or indifferent. The pressure is all self-induced. The reality is it's okay. I studied Deepak Chopra and what I learned is that there is no such thing as good or bad luck, it's how you approach it. You are going to get good bounces and you are going to get bad bounces—and that is the way it is.

Are you superstitious at all?

In a way, but I don't go crazy about it. I don't like yellow. I never used a yellow tee. No special shirts, coins or anything like that.

Do you have intrusive thoughts or negative thoughts? Or is your mind constantly positive and full of confidence? Or, even better, is your mind able to go blank?

We all have moments of doubt. Pressure is all about controlling your emotional makeup and your muscular makeup, which comes into timing and rhythm. I remember one tournament at

PGA West, I was saying to myself, "What am I going to hit on eighteen if I have a one shot lead?" So thoughts like that swirl a lot.

On a scale of 1-10, with 10 being the highest, how confident would you say you are on the golf course?

When I turned fifty and won two tournaments in a row, I was a 10. I would look up and down the range and I would say there is no way these people will beat me. When I turned fifty-six more people came out and put more pressure on me. It is easy to lose confidence. When I was in my late fifties, I lost my confidence.

What do you think of sports psychology as a whole? Do you think it is legitimate or BS?

All psychology is stuff that we already know but may have forgotten. If you don't have a good routine, go get a good routine. Try to visualize the shot of the ball. It is stuff that reminds you of what to do and how to do it. I don't think it's bogus. If it does what you feel you need then you should go with it. Everybody is very different. I kind of dabbled in it. Some golfers talked to their sports psychologist every day—I don't think I needed that.

Bruce then told me a story about when he was he playing a practice round with Ben Crenshaw and Fuzzy Zoeller:

There were two people watching and I heard them say, "Here is Ben Crenshaw and Fuzzy Zoeller, then here is Fleisher, what a bum." So I went over to them and said, "I have been around the world five times, met kings and queens, I never considered myself a bum." I walked away and I thought I had educated them. As I walked away I heard them say, "He is still a bum." You are not going to satisfy everyone.

Do you think about your score when on the golf course? Do you look at the scoreboards?

Yeah, I knew what I was shooting. I was always aware, especially if I was in the hunt. I always wanted to know where I was. Some people don't look at the scoreboard, which I found kind of odd.

Do you get nervous during tournaments or practice for what seems like no reason at all?

Certainly not practicing. I think you want to get nervous; it means you are attuned and focusing. If you're not nervous, you're not going to play well. There are different types of nervousness. There is scared nervousness and there is confident nervousness. I describe confident nervousness as you're doing your routine well, your breathing is good, and you're focused. I studied Nicklaus and tried to emulate him.

Are there any people that you felt like it was harder to play in front of, such as somebody you knew in the crowd?

I struggled with this. If somebody started with me, I was fine; if they came in the middle of the round, it bugged the crap out of me—I hated it. My psychologist told me you have to learn to welcome these people. They are coming to support you. They are not there to fight you. What it really did was unfocus me, and I didn't like it. I would tell people, "If you are going to come and watch me, come at the beginning." Then I would be fine. But when they would come in the middle of the round and wanted to be recognized, I hated it. It just really threw me off. I was eventually able to train myself to say they are here to support me and to enjoy me so let me enjoy them as well. Let's face it, if you are totally focused and then someone gets in your face and makes you lose even one percent of your focus, it is not a good thing. I really had to train myself to drown it out. I think we[26] fight it because our character is weak in that area. I can't quite put a finger on it, or why it happens, but it has to be a flaw in our makeup.

What do you think it takes to make it as a professional golfer?

It is a scoring game. You got to do it all. You have to keep in play, you have to control your ball, and you have to putt. My success came within one hundred yards. I was the best with my wedges on the Senior Tour. I was sixty-fourth in driving distance, yet I was number one in birdie conversions on par 5s simply because I was so good with my wedges. I knew them to the nth degree. I would tell people to learn to hit your wedges, learn to chip, and learn to putt.

In your opinion what do you think is the ideal mindset for a golfer?

Really focus on getting out of the box. Whether that is good breathing, good routine, or good walking. Really concentrate on

---

[26] By "we" he meant him and me because I told him I had a similar issue.

the first few holes. Don't want to get behind the eight-ball early. I would focus on grinding it out early.

What do you feel changed for you from the PGA Tour to the Champions Tour that allowed you to be more successful?

Playing through my forties; I was the straightest driver on Tour; timing, fate, and never giving up. I had three to five years where nobody could really beat me. I was competitively ready. When the golfers who had a lot of success on the PGA Tour tried to get back on the Senior Tour after being retired for about eight years, they were not ready—and I was.

POSITIVE TAKEAWAYS

▶ I liked that Bruce told me that a big part of his motivation was money and wanting to be comfortable. I feel we live in a world where people look down on people who do things for money. Bruce was sick of making $50K annually, so with the support of a backer he did something about it and made a boatload of money. From 1999 to 2004, he made more than $12 million on the Senior Tour. This contradicts what Chip Beck said. Chip thought it wasn't good to play for the money, but it worked for Bruce. This just furthers illustrates my point of how **there is no right or wrong** mindset about golf. People can think differently and be successful.

▶ I loved how he disagreed that people should always visualize their success and watch their successes, a common theory by golf psychologists. This is in direct conflict with what Mr. O told me. According to Mr. O's logic, golfers should watch tapes of themselves winning because it will help increase the self-image. Better yet, Bruce told me that some of golf's greatest—Lee Trevino, Arnold Palmer, and Ray Floyd—never watched themselves because they would be their own worst critic.

▶ I thought it was interesting how Bruce didn't describe himself as the most competitive person. He wasn't driven to be the best—he just wanted to make a living. I often hear in today's sporting world how athletes are so competitive and hate to lose more than anything. In Bruce's own words he "just wanted to make money and did not really care about being the best." I respect him a lot for saying that. Despite not being the most competitive person, he was unstoppable for about five years.

▶ I found it very interesting when Bruce got into talking about people he didn't like. I think it is very important for readers to take note of this. One reason is that the media and the overall perception of golf is that everybody is so nice to each other. However, I learned from Bruce's stories that there are some dirt bags out there who will try to distract others just to get what they feel is an edge. Whether that is standing in people's lines or trying to rattle other players.

▶ I liked what Bruce said about pressure and how it's all self-induced. Pressure is all about controlling your emotional makeup, and, more importantly, your muscular makeup which comes into timing and rhythm. That was something I struggled with. I would get so shaky that it was very hard to have feel—and that is a big issue for a golfer.

▶ I felt Bruce's story where he defended himself to the people who called him a bum was important because it shows that you can't make everyone like or respect you regardless of whether you are a high profile person or not. You need to have thick skin and let a lot of things go. It is very relatable to Gonzalo's comments about how it is impossible to please everyone.

▶ My favorite part of this interview was when he discussed how he struggled when people he knew would pop up in the middle of rounds to watch him. This struck a very personal chord for me; it made me feel better that someone as successful as Bruce had the same issue I had. The difference is that he was able to train himself to get over the problem, while I could never really get over it. This is an issue that I believe serious golfers have to get over or not have in the first place to make it professionally. Because, let's face it, there's always going to be someone you know watching. I think Bruce really hit the nail on the head when he described this issue as "our character being weak in that area." There is no real reason why we have that issue, it's just a part of our makeup. He made me feel more normal about that issue, whereas the golf psychologists made me feel like I was the only person on the planet who struggled with it and that there was a simple cure. It took Bruce a long time to figure out how to drown that out. It is much easier said than done. Irrational flaws, fears, or whatever you want to call them are so frustrating because in your mind you know they are ridiculous. At the same time, it's hard to get what I would describe as your "being" to understand it to the point where the issue no longer persists.

NEGATIVE TAKEAWAYS

▶ The fact that he felt like it was especially important to start out of the box well. I thoroughly believe that every shot, every hole, and every round are equally important.

▶ I don't agree that you need to feel nervous to play well. Of course you can play well being nervous, but there is no reason why a golfer can't play well calm.

I really enjoyed talking with Bruce; he was very open with everything. His story is very unique in the fact that he had at best a mediocre PGA Tour career and then a hall of fame career on the Senior Tour.

HALE IRWIN

CAREER HIGHLIGHTS

- Highest World Golf Ranking: 2
- 1967 NCAA Champion
- Roughly $6 million on PGA Tour
- Roughly $27 million on Champions Tour
- Twenty PGA Tour Victories, 25 runner-up finishes, 165 top 10s
- Three-time US Open Champion (1974, 1979, and 1990)
- Forty-five Champions Tour Victories, 43 runner-up finishes

- Five Ryder cup teams
- Has won golf tournaments in six continents

INTERVIEW QUESTIONS

Do you love to show off how good you are?

No, I don't think that is appropriate. I never had any desire to prove anything to the outside world. I just wanted to please myself and I was always my own hardest critic.

Have you ever seen a sports psychologist or shrink for golf? If yes, what did you talk about or work on?

No, but I have had several come to me and ask questions about the way that I think. My belief is that there is some good advice coming from those people. I may not always agree with them and all of their messages, but I have never worked with one.

What motivated you to get the point where you are at? To be the best? Money? Something else?

I've always had competitive instincts to want to get better in all the sports I played. As I got older, I definitely enjoyed my successes. I excelled in the athletic world. Definitely couldn't say the same about the academic world.

What was your economic status growing up?

Wasn't very pretty. I grew up in a city where Mickey Mantle was a big influence, so baseball was the biggest sport in my town. In my town there was only a 9-hole golf course where the greens were all sand and there was no irrigation system. My dad built me some clubs and wrapped them in electrical tape. Both my mom and dad worked, so when I was offered a full football scholarship to CU, I jumped on it. We always had food on the table and love from our parents, which was all that really mattered.

Did you ever get uncomfortable when you were doing really well, like -5 in a round?

No, I did not get uncomfortable during those times. I always wanted to go more under par. If I was at -4, I wanted to get to -5, then to -6, and so forth. It's fun when you're playing well, you just want to keep going. What made me more uncomfortable were the physical settings. For example, when I was wearing glasses in the British Open, that was tough for me. Most of my better tournaments were in better conditions. So the physical conditions made me more uncomfortable than my mental conditions.

Do you talk trash at all on the golf course? Do you know any players who do?

No. No place for that. Lee Trevino just talked—didn't talk trash, but just liked to talk. He didn't care if you responded or not—he just talked. When I looked at my pairings and saw who I was paired with,

I just got prepared accordingly depending on who I was playing with, such as I was going to have a slow day, a noisy day, or a quiet day. I feel like people who talk trash will have it come back and bite them.

Which parent encouraged or pushed you with golf? What did this parent/parents instill in you?

My father got me started along with other sports. My mom supported me as well. In my home town there was not much to do. Kids found their own activities and I gravitated toward sports. Baseball was my most natural sport. What I liked about golf was that I could just go out and play by myself. I didn't need someone to play catch with or teammates to get a game going. When I moved to Colorado around fourteen years old, I played in a junior tournament and it was one of three times I played on grass greens since the course I grew up on was mostly sand. I was surprised that I won the tournament and it was exhilarating. That really got me going with golf. I would caddie, then I used that money for greens fees.

Did you get into a certain mindset before your rounds? For example: "I'm gonna tear these people apart;" "I'm gonna set the course record today;" "I'm never going back to the mini tours." Or something completely different?

No, not really. I was mature enough and I had enough experience in the game to know that there were better players than me. But that is not what makes a good golfer. The way to be a good golfer, in my opinion, is to remain mentally neutral, to not get too charged, excited, or down. I did not worry about others, I just focused on my game and didn't want to be counterproductive.

Were you ever intimidated by an opponent or did any opponents ever make you feel uncomfortable?

No never intimidated. I always wanted to play with the best. I wanted to play with Nicklaus or Palmer. I enjoyed playing with those guys. I learned from their presence in terms of how to act and react. You see why they are the best players and why they are successful. You can take things from other players and try to incorporate it in your game. For example, I saw that Nicklaus was teeing it up higher than I was off the tee, so I experimented with that for a while. I tried to absorb everything I could and incorporate the things that made sense to me in my game.

When did you know you were good enough to make it?

I don't know tomorrow. It was never a revelation. Maybe winning NCAAs was the catalyst to get me to turn pro. After I graduated I got one of fifteen PGA Tour cards. When you get out there you see how good these players are and you mature very quickly in terms of both your game and mind.

Do you have intrusive thoughts or negative thoughts? Or is your mind constantly positive and full of confidence? Or, even better, is your mind able to go blank?

It's impossible to not have negative thoughts. You wouldn't be human if you didn't. But I tried to push them aside. Here is an example: my dad was dying during the 1984 US Open, so I created a scenario where I could do this monumental thing of winning the US Open and it might be one of the last things my dad gets to see. I got to trying too hard for my dad. I made it a big mountain and didn't do as well as I should have. The game of golf can create a lot of negative tension, but I tried not to focus on it. For example, you could feel negative one day hitting the ball and the next day could be a total 180.

On a scale of 1-10, with 10 being the highest, how confident would you say you are on the golf course?

I would love to say a 10, but that would be unrealistic. I would say an 8 and then work from there. You do have to take a realism pill and know that you will not always be confident. If I hit a tree, I always expected the ball to bounce in the fairway. I expected good performance from myself and was not pleased with poor performance.

What do you think of sports psychology as a whole? Do you think it is legitimate or BS?

I think there is some good advice coming from these people but it depends on the individual receiving the information. Does it make them a better player? Does it deeply change their attitudes? These are questions you need to ask. Do I think it is a lot of hype? Yes. I overheard a shrink say focus on a leaf. I feel like that is setting yourself up for failure, because I will fail if I am trying to hit a leaf. I just say hit the fairway. Pretty narrow-minded to hit a leaf in my opinion. At the same time this was not directed toward me so it's tough for me to say. You really need to find your comfort zone and what works for you.

Was the field of sports psychology around in your era?

No, it didn't exist. A lady from Texas was the first person to ask me how I thought.

Do you think about your score when on the golf course? Do you look at the scoreboards?

I liked to see what was going on. To turn your mind away from what is going on is ridiculous to me. I think it is very important to know where you stand. I would give myself time to detach in between shots, then, when I got closer to the ball, I reeled it back in. To be out there for all those hours and to only think about golf is crazy. There is too much idle time to only think about golf. Even if I was not doing well I would allow myself to look at the scoreboards just for the pure entertainment of seeing who was winning.

Do you get nervous during tournaments or practice for what seems like no reason at all?

No, not really. For some players when they play well they get anxiety, it quickens their mind. I turned my nerves into good nerves. For some people, nerves made them sharper. It can go the other way very quickly though. If I got negative, I tried to get off it.

Hale then went into talking about how things outside of golf can affect you and how he dealt with it:

It is against human nature to not focus on some things. You have to find your own way on how to deal with that.

When issues outside of golf were troubling him, he would give himself thirty seconds to think about whatever it was, then— when it came time to hit the shot—he was able to reel in his mind and get focused again. He also discussed body language, how it's so overrated and talked about too much. He said, Pete Sampras looked like he could barely make it to the next point when he played tennis, but he was obviously a great champion. You have to find your own way and what works for you.

Are there any people that you felt like it was harder to play in front of, such as somebody you knew in the crowd?

No. Having reached my level of success I have had the opportunity to play with some very famous and powerful people. They are just people like you and me. There are no super humans out there and nobody is Superman. When I played, I was able to get into my own isolated capsule and was not worried about who was there and who wasn't.

Do you feel that your football experiences helped you become a better golfer in anyway? If so how?

Football gave me a lot of discipline. What goes into preparing for a football season takes a lot of discipline. My senior year, I was captain of the football team and I wanted to be a leader that really emphasized never giving up. I was not a rah-rah-type of captain. I liked to lead by example. I just tried to do my best each and every down. I believe that training with other sports helped my golf and golf helped with the other sports. I was able to translate this into golf because I played golf in the current moment and was able to get over shots quickly. I learned to do your best today and do better tomorrow. I knew what I had to do to get better and that was what I did.

In addition, I was undersized with football, so I had to do other things to make up for that. For example, I wasn't going to outhit other players or be the fastest so I had to do something better than other people. I have taken that mentality to golf.

In your opinion what do you think it takes to make it as a professional golfer?

You need to have a deep seated desire to want to be successful. I see a lot of younger people these days and I think they are coddled. People in their hometown, city, state, etc., tell them how great they are and they don't realize that there are people all over the world trying to be better than them. You need a deep belief in yourself. Nothing is handed to you, you have to work hard for things. If it something worth having, you've got to work for it. Have to be mature. Golf is about more than just hitting the ball. A lot of people can hit the ball very well but, for whatever reason, they don't make it. Perhaps they didn't have the comfort of being away from home. Or maybe they were not comfortable with living in the tense times that come with being a pro golfer. There are also people who win big tournaments and then you never hear from them again because they forget how they got there.

Can you tell me the story about Seve in the Ryder Cup when he said to you, "I wish you hit it in the water?"

At the 1991 Ryder Cup at Kiwah Island, I was playing against Bernhard Langer in a close match on the last day and the cup depended on our match. The seventeenth hole at Kiwah is a par-3 with water short of the green. So on the seventeenth hole, after Bernhard and I hit our tee shots, I heard Seve say something in Spanish to another one of the European players. To ease the tension a little bit for myself I went over to ask Seve what he said. Seve said, "It's too bad you didn't hit it in the water." If there was anybody to get under your skin, it was him. He didn't care much for Americans. He came from a different background. **I wanted to tell this story as it demonstrates how golfers aren't necessarily angels who constantly wish each other well.**

POSITIVE TAKEAWAYS

It's quite clear that Hale has an incredibly strong mind. I suppose that comes with the territory of being a hall of fame golfer.

▶ I obviously liked the fact that Hale has never seen a sports psychologist. It definitely helps prove my point that you do not need a "mental coach" to be a successful golfer.

▶ I liked Hale's mentality of always wanting to go lower and lower in a round when he was playing well.

▶ I love the fact that Hale was never intimidated by anyone. In golf, you don't have time to pick and choose who you will be intimidated by. From a purely rationale perspective it doesn't matter who you play with or who is around—the shots don't change—however, that was something I struggled with. Hale said something profound about playing golf in front others: he has played golf with a lot of powerful individuals, but in the end we are all humans. I believe we give other people so much power, or place too much importance on them, when there is no reason to. We are all no better or worse than anyone else and there is no real reason to get intimidated or uncomfortable in front of anyone. At least that's true rationally.

▶ It's excellent how Hale says it's impossible to not have negative thoughts. You would not be human if you didn't have these thoughts. I wish that Dr. BS would have heard Hale say this because he made me feel like there was something wrong with me for having negative and intrusive thoughts.

▶ That he liked to look at leaderboards because it's important to know where you stand.

▶ How body language is overanalyzed. For example, he illustrated how Pete Sampras looked very sluggish when he played. The same thing can be said about Jason Dufner; he always looks like he is moping around, but it obviously works for him.

▶ My favorite thing Hale talked about was how things outside of golf can affect your game. The way that he dealt with it was allowing himself to think about whatever the issue was for thirty seconds, then when he approached the shot he would refocus. To me that is an unbelievable ability. If I had that ability, things outside of golf would not have affected me nearly as much as they did. I think it is one of the most impressive abilities of Hale.

▶ In summary, Hale hits the nail on the head when he says, "You have to find your own way and what works for you." Or as I like to say **there is no right or wrong.**

NEGATIVE TAKEAWAYS

I don't have any and I think we can all learn a lot from what Hale had to say.

JONATHON KAYE

CAREER HIGHLIGHTS

- Highest World Golf Ranking: 14
- Roughly $10.5 million in career earnings on PGA Tour
- Two PGA Tour victories
- Eight runner-up finishes, and 31 top 10 finishes

INTERVIEW QUESTIONS

Do you love to show off how good you are?

I love to show off when I know I am hitting it good. Right now I wouldn't be showing anything off. When I was competing, I would love to show off. There were times when I would find someone who didn't even want a challenge and I would challenge them.

Have you ever seen a sports psychologist or shrink for golf? If yes, what did you talk about or work on?

Never as a professional. In college my coach brought in a guy to work with the team and he said deep breathing and things of that nature. He turned out to be a fraud though. I have never paid for any sports psychology.

What motivated you to get to the point where you are at? To be the best? Money? Something else?

It was easy for me. I didn't want to get a job in an office and make a small salary. I said to myself that I would give myself three years to make it as a pro, and if I didn't make it, I would do something else. I got lucky and I got through Q-School in my second year.

What was your economic status growing up?

I was upper middle class, but never belonged to any country clubs.

Did you ever get uncomfortable when you were doing really well, like -5 in a round?

No, of course not. Why would you get nervous? I was always thinking, "Let me get to -6, -7, -8, and so forth." Those are the days that are fun. When I got to the last hole on those days I was upset that there were no more holes to play and make more birdies.

Do you talk trash at all on the golf course? Do you know any players who do?

Not regularly. I mean I have no problem being quiet but with certain players I liked to. Not necessarily ill-willed things but I like to talk trash. The guy I talked the most shit to was Vijay—I would just roast him. **Here are a couple of stories describing their banter.** I was once playing with Vijay in the WGC in Akron, Ohio, and we both shot something around -1 on the front nine. Then on our eleventh hole, I said to him, "Hey Vijay, I bet Phil could kick your ass." **Jonathan told me that Vijay and Phil did not like each other because Phil wore metal spikes or something along those lines. That morning Jonathan saw Phil doing taekwondo in the parking lot, or some form of exercise, and that is why he said he could kick Vijay's ass.** Vijay then said, "I would kick that guy's ass." Jonathan said he lit a fire under Vijay. He bombed a drive on that hole and had nine iron into a par-5, then played really well the rest of the round. So Vijay fed off of my shit sometimes. I'm sure he talked plenty to me as well. I like talking shit, it's fun. **Here is some other banter.** Vijay would sometimes say, "I am going to outdrive you this hole."

I would respond saying "Yeah, you better—you're 6'4" and weigh 235 pounds. I weigh 155 soaking wet." Then I would say things like, "Vijay you have a receding hairline." Or if there was a girl following the group I would joke with him saying, "Is that your woman following you?"

Which parent encouraged or pushed you with golf? What did this parent/parents instill in you?

My grandfather. He just told me to never get mad, it's just a game. My dad had a terrible temper on the golf course, he could not get through a round without breaking half of his set.

When warming up on the range before a round what are your thoughts? For example: "I'm gonna tear these people apart;" "I'm gonna set the course record today;" "I'm never going back to the mini tours." Or something completely different?

When I was warming up I was just focused on what my shots were doing on the range. If I was hooking it on the range, I would play that. My mindset was when I looked at where I stood after a round, I would look at the score that was ahead of me and chase that. For example, if I was five shots out of a top ten I would say, "OK, I can get there." I never concerned myself with who or what was behind me. I have always had a very aggressive mindset and was never really concerned with the consequences.

Were you ever intimidated by an opponent or did any opponents ever make you feel uncomfortable?

I was never intimidated by anyone in an emotional sense. But I was intimidated in some sense when I would see some of the shots that some of these players would hit and I knew I could not hit those types of shots. For example, I have never been able to bomb the ball and some of these guys just pound it. But I would say screw them, I will just make more putts than them. I relished the challenge.

When did you know you were good enough to make it?

I never really thought that way. If you asked some of my college teammates what they were going to do after school, they would have said they were going to be on the PGA Tour. I never really cared if I succeeded at golf. If you had asked me what I was going to do, I would have told you I have no idea. In that sense I believe some of my teammates could not get out of their own way. One thing that I feel is necessary in order to "make it" is being able to make changes. For example, before I turned pro I just played a draw. I made changes and learned how to hit a fade. Once I started to compete in tournaments to win, I started to know I was good enough. There is a big learning curve, such as getting used to course conditions.

Do you have intrusive thoughts or negative thoughts? Or is your mind constantly positive and full of confidence? Or, even better, is your mind able to go blank?

I had tons of negative thoughts. I try to be positive. Every time I hit a bad shot it was because of a negative thought.

On a scale of 1-10, with 10 being the highest, how confident would you say you are on the golf course?

I would give myself a 9. I was always confident in my abilities. I felt that if I played average I would be OK. The more you play, the more you figure out how to make your bad rounds better.

What do you think of sports psychology as a whole? Do you think it is legitimate or BS?

I kind of see it like religion. If you can drink the Kool-Aid and have an open mind, then it can help you. I don't believe in it, but I can respect people who do believe in it.

Do you think about your score when on the golf course? Do you look at the scoreboards?

A little bit. It's hard not to, they're in your face. I liked to know where I was in regards to the cut line. I thought about money, not when I was playing a round—but money made me realize that there were ramifications for certain decisions. So while I didn't think about it on the golf course, it influenced future decisions very quickly.

Do you get nervous during tournaments or practice for what seems like no reason at all?

On the first tee I would get nervous. I had a fear of duffing it. But I liked it. I felt like it was the competitive juices flowing. I believe there is a lot of weight on that first tee shot. I almost felt a little claustrophobic on the first tee and, once I got out of there, I felt fine.

Are there any people that you felt like it was harder to play in front of, such as someone you knew in the crowd?

No. I never had a fear of judgement from people I know. When I was struggling, I would maybe get that judgement feeling, but not really.

What do you think it takes to make it as a professional golfer?

A really short memory. Talent. You can't be taught to be a great golfer. It can't be taught; it is either born with you or not.

I remember you telling me stories from the US Open where you cursed someone out and how you left practice one day because it went over the twenty hours . . . Can you tell me those again?

I hit it in a bunker on one of the first holes at the US Open and ended up in a footprint. I then hit it in another bunker and was in another footprint. I got really pissed off, because to have this happen two times in four holes is just ridiculous. So when I crossed paths with the group ahead of ours on one of the next few holes, I let them have it. I mean just cursed them out furiously. Cause keeping it on the green at the US Open is hard enough. I don't need to deal with footprints on top of that.

During one of my years in school, the NCAA instituted the twenty hours a week of practice rule. So one week I counted the hours and the twentieth hour hit when I was on the fifteenth hole at Boulder Country Club during qualifying. I said, "My twenty hours are up—see ya!" and I walked off the course. I didn't care if I went on that trip. There were certain ones I cared about and others I didn't. I was sick of spending so much time on the course. I wanted to have more time to myself. I never went on spring break trips with the golf team. I wanted a spring break to myself. If I was on full scholarship, maybe I would have felt more obligated. There was a tournament at Stanford where the groups played with all five members of their team in the actual tournament. On the ninth hole I broke my putter, but nobody saw me break it. So on our tenth hole I was putting for eagle and I brought my wedge to putt. My coach said, "What are you doing? Go get your putter." I responded saying, "I have been putting badly so I am going to try this." My coach then said, "Get your putter again," so I went to my bag and pulled out the two pieces of the putter. Once my coach saw that he picked up my ball from the green and said, "We won't be needing your services anymore." He didn't tell me anything after that. So I went to the clubhouse and saw Notah Begay, who was redshirting that year. He gave me a ride back to the hotel, I called a cab at the hotel, bought a twelve-pack and ordered a pizza. When the coach saw me in the hotel he said, "Where the hell have you been? We have been looking all over for you." And I responded, "I've been here drinking beer. You should have told me where to go. Did you really expect me to sit in the clubhouse and do nothing? I'm a big boy and can get around town."

Feel free to add any comments or thoughts about anything golf-related or not.

What I love about golf is that it is an unbiased game. It doesn't matter who you are or where you come from. If you can hit shots at the pin and get the ball in the hole, it doesn't matter who you are. Also, I am so glad that I never had a boss or anyone to answer to. That is something I would not have been good at. At this point in my life I don't really need to play golf anymore. I do have status on the Web.com Tour, but I can't see myself doing the Web.com Tour, traveling to South America, leaving my family and possibly losing $3,000.

POSITIVE TAKEAWAYS

I have to start off by saying that Jonathon is my favorite golfer. As I said earlier in the book, it just so happened that I got to know him a little when I was randomly paired to play with him and his wife one day in Colorado. I just loved his attitude. It was a recreational round but he was talking smack, annoying his wife, and having a blast on the course.

The reason that Jonathon is my favorite golfer is because I know that I needed to emulate his attitude more if I was going to be a successful golfer. The two main things would be not caring at all and marching to the beat of my own drum.

▶ First off—as always—I like that Jonathon has not seen a sports psychologist and had a successful PGA Tour career. Just like Hale, when he was playing well, he relished the day and wanted to go as low as possible. He thought I was crazy for even asking him if he got nervous when he was playing well.

▶ I liked how Jonathon liked to mess around and joke with certain people he was playing with. I thought the stories he told about talking trash with Vijay were hysterical.

▶ I loved how Jonathon described his motivation for golf. The simple fact was that it was easy for him and he wanted to make a lot of money. It's a very honest answer.

▶ It's clear that Jonathon was very confident in his abilities, saying that he usually felt around a 9 on a scale of 1-10, and that if he played ok he would be alright.

▶ I liked how Jonathon said he thought about score in regards to the cut line. This seems to be a fairly common theme amongst the golfers I interviewed. Most are more concerned with the cutline than anything else—and rightfully so. If a golfer doesn't make the cut, they aren't going to make any prize money that week. So, in reality, the first two days are the most important.

Obviously, Jonathon's stories are entertaining. But besides their entertainment value, I believe there are valuable lessons that can be drawn from them. His first story about how he yelled at somebody for not raking the bunker is valuable for the following reasons:

▶ It's important to not be a pushover and be able to stand your ground. Chip Beck touched on this point as well.

▶ The second story about him walking off the course in college is important to me, not because I agree with what he did, but because of his mindset: Jonathon does not care about what anybody thinks. This is something I struggled with in golf. I was always concerned with what people thought of my game and it affected me in a negative way. In golf, the less you care, the better, for the most part. In college, my coach told me a story about three friends who played golf together. They either grew up with each other or played college golf together. The specifics don't really matter. They were all pretty good golfers, but the one who actually had a successful professional career was the worst of the three. So this individual was asked one day why he did better than his two friends who were more talented than him. His response was, "I tried like hell, but I didn't give a shit." To put it in a different perspective, if a student has a test, they should prepare for the test as hard as they can, but once it comes time to take the test they need to let go and not care at all. Jonathan is a perfect example of trying his best, but still not caring. That's a very powerful attitude.

NEGATIVE TAKEAWAYS

▶ I don't agree with Jonathon that there's a lot of weight on the first tee shot. All shots are the same and equally important.

▶ To some extent, his actions are too ridiculous and I don't necessarily agree with them, although I certainly respect the hell out of him for being so bold. He had an obligation in college to his team and he should have taken it more seriously.

JASON BURSTYN

CHAPTER 7

Conclusion

Some of my golfing heroes are Patrick Reed, Jonathon Kaye, Brooks Koepka, and Tiger Woods—but my biggest hero of all is Howard Stern. You might be asking yourself why Howard Stern? What I admire most about him is that he was a pioneer, a trailblazer who revolutionized the radio industry. How did he do this? Well, in my opinion, he went completely against the grain of what was considered "right" or "acceptable." He challenged the zeitgeist. He started to say what was on his mind no matter how many feathers he ruffled, no matter how many fines he got from the Federal Communications Commission, and no matter how many people he offended. For that, he is my biggest hero and a big inspiration to me.

I feel this book I have written will challenge the status quo of what is perceived as "right" or "acceptable" in the game of golf. I know that people are going to have different reactions to and opinions of my book. In all honesty, I don't care if people hate it. Some people might think I am wrong, and that's fine. It was important for me to express myself, and tell it the way I see it—just like Howard.

So how about the other people on that list. Why are they my heroes? Now, in my opinion, the other people on the list fall in the same category as Howard. They all go against the grain of what is common or cliché, do what they want, and march to the beat of their own drum.

People reading this book may say, "Jason Burstyn is a case of sour grapes; he's going around blaming sports psychologists for his problems when he just can't face the simple truth that he wasn't good enough." Nothing could be further from the truth. I didn't reach my full potential because I didn't have the mental side of golf for whatever reason. Too many things rattled me. Whether people want to call it not having "it" or that "X factor," a self-image issue, lack of confidence or belief. I don't know. But neither do psychologists. My father and I searched high and low for solutions to my irrational thinking/feelings on the golf course. For the most part, there was nothing the shrinks said that ever made me feel better. In fact, they hurt more than helped. Golf shrinks led me to believe that my mind was flawed because I had certain thoughts or my mind wandered.

I needed to be my own authority of what was right or wrong. I now know what I needed to be: more confident, harder, competitive, and an emotional rock. I needed the mentality of me against the world. But, the real question is, what did I need to do to become that way? Did I need to be cut off financially so there was no safety net? Did I need to care less? Did I need to accept the fact that I might become a bum? I don't know. Every person is an individual and they need to figure out what works for them. But, in my opinion, this cookie-cutter approach that sports psychology offers certainly isn't what works. Be who you want to be as a golfer. Don't let anyone tell you what is right or wrong. If you want to smile on the golf course—then smile. If you want to be emotionless on the golf course—do that. If you want to have swing thoughts—have them. If you want to talk trash on the golf course—talk trash. If you want to think about score—then think about score. If you want to think about money—then think about money. **There is no right or wrong!**

I don't know how these golf psychologists have gone on for as long as they have without anyone really questioning them. They go unchallenged on a subject that is inherently "mysterious," speak about the mind as if certain things are fact or set in stone, and present generic solutions for golfers' mental struggles. From what I have observed they speak in generalities and do not provide any evidence that I would consider conclusive. If a golf shrink could somehow definitively show that players advised by golf psychology professionals outperform those who have not received "mental training," I would be able to accept the validity of the field. Unfortunately, I'm not sure how that would be possible. These psychologists have a lot of anecdotal evidence, which isn't irrelevant, but there is plenty of other anecdotal evidence that contradicts their theories which I provided. These shrinks have become validated because PGA Tour players work with them. However, just because famous people work with an individual doesn't make them credible. Maybe the shrinks did help the golfers they worked with and maybe they didn't. Correlation doesn't necessarily explain causation. Just because some successful pro golfers saw these shrinks doesn't mean that was the causation of their success. The bottom line is that these golfers were great before they saw sports psychologists, and they probably would have been great had they not seen them. Let me ask you this: how is it possible that golfers from the past could have been great champions without sports psychology? How did Ben Hogan, Gene Sarazon, or Bobby Jones win without shrinks? It's possible they saw some version of a sports psychologist, but I highly doubt it.

I would also like to clarify that I don't have a special grudge against Dr. Bob Rotella even though he is the main focal point in my book. It's just that he is the leader of golf psychology and is very well published. I have issues with golf psychologists as a whole since they overall preach the same message and piggy back off of each other. In the last few years, I came to a very profound realization: just because someone is "an expert"—whether that be a psychologist, lawyer, doctor, physical therapist, financial advisor, etc.—doesn't mean they have all the answers, if any at all. It doesn't mean you should take what they say at face value. I should have challenged the information that was presented to me so many times, but I accepted what I was told at face value because I was listening to "the experts" and hoping they could help me. Perhaps I was hyper gullible and I wanted to believe just about anything since I knew I needed help.

Let me clarify that, although I am a stubborn person, I am not close-minded. Because of my experiences, however, I have developed a heavy dose of skepticism to theories or sales pitches. A person should not go through life close-minded or else they will never learn anything, but people need to be careful about information that is presented to them and take a hard look at it before accepting it.

So folks, if you thought I was going to give you the answers to the mind or a guide to a mental approach, I am sorry to disappoint, but I don't have them. I don't have the solution to filter out unwanted thoughts, crazy theories, superstitions, self-imposed limitations, fears, or how to gain confidence. Nobody does!

However, I certainly do have suggestions. Golfers of all ages need to figure out what works for them. They shouldn't be lemmings and see sports psychologists just because Tour pros do or because it has been validated by golf culture. I have presented a different perspective of sports psychology to help you make better informed decisions if you really want to invest time and money in this industry for yourself or someone else. Obviously, I would never suggest this to anyone because—as I have detailed throughout this book—I believe a majority of what they say is flawed. Just because that is my opinion, doesn't mean it has to be yours. Once again do what works for you! **There is no right or wrong** with golf in terms of a mental approach/thinking. You should be able to gather that based on the interviews that I conducted. For the most part, my interviewees had different experiences and went about things differently. Some saw certain situations as stressful, while others did not. Some got nervous when playing well and some did not. Some saw golf psychologists and some did not. Some liked to have people they know watching them and some did not. Some liked to think about money and some did not. Get the picture. No two people are alike and there cannot be a single standardized approach to the mind. As Socrates said, "Know thyself."

That's why it was so important for me to get those interviews with world-class golfers. Not all of them think the same. Pick someone whose personality works for you, a combination, or don't emulate any of them. As I have been preaching: **there is no right or wrong**.

In all honesty, people can get mental advice from anyone, not just "experts"—just like Compton felt his swing instructor was a "psychologist" of sorts. It goes to show, that golfers don't necessarily need to pay "qualified individuals" to tell them the "right" way to think.

Jonathon Kaye was like that for me. He is certainly not a psychologist, but what he said and his overall attitude towards golf made me a mentally stronger person—at least for a couple of months.

Another reason for writing this book is I want aspiring junior/college-aged golfers and their parents to learn from my experiences so that they can make better golf and life decisions. Teenagers and young adults have to realize the opportunity cost that occurs when they are extremely dedicated to golf, because at the end of the day, it's their lives and they are the ones who have to live with their choices and decisions. They are potentially going to be the ones who fall behind in the job market, become one-dimensional, and have minimal experiences in the world. As a result, I believe kids who are talented at a young age at golf should absolutely work at the game, get better at it, and see where it takes them. However, it's important that they treat it as a game. It's important that junior golfers be well-rounded people and not have horse blinders on with their sole focus being golf. They can concentrate on golf, but there is no reason they shouldn't also focus on friendships, relationships, academics, or other hobbies. Because all of those things take time, a teenager should be spending a maximum of sixteen hours a week on golf—and even that is a lot of time.

To my fellow mini tour golfers who have been grinding for entirely too long without seeing any profits come their way, let me clarify that I am not here to diminish golfers' dreams of trying to make it to the PGA Tour. Everybody has the right to turn pro and try to make it. If no one tried, there wouldn't be any Zach Johnsons who got better after college and ended up making it. But, from my experience, golfers who don't make honest assessments of their game suffer in their lives as a consequence. I play golf with an incredibly successful attorney I met through my dad; he has become a friend and confidant and explained to me when I stopped playing golf that what you do in life isn't that important. It's just a means to an end. That is my suggestion to a vast majority of the golfers who have no business playing professional golf. There are a thousand different ways to make money. Golf is not the only one, so you should probably start figuring out another way to make money. Your job does not define who you are, it's simply a tool to allow you to live a certain lifestyle and hopefully achieve some comfort.

I'm happy I moved on from golf. I went back to school the year after I stopped playing and graduated with a Master's degree in Finance from the University of Miami. I got to travel and go on some spectacular group trips to Israel and Brazil. On both trips I was with about forty-five other people my age, cruising around the country and partying. They were some of the best times of my life. My first job out of school was in the alcohol industry. Overall I like working. It's nice to make a steady paycheck and to feel some stability in my life, although I wouldn't say it's guaranteed. You still have to perform, but it is definitely better than gambling on mini tours. The corporate world is very competitive and unlike golf it is not necessarily based on merit in the sense that the best person gets the job or that they're in control of their destiny. With that said, I am living proof that there is life beyond golf and there are a lot of opportunities.

In terms of playing golf nowadays, I don't play competitively that often. I play with a group most Saturday mornings and give golf lessons on the side during weekends, which I thoroughly enjoy. As for professional golf, I made a vow to myself that I wouldn't give it another shot unless two things happened: first, I would have to lose all of my irrational thinking, limitations, and phobias; second, I need to get five years of work experience under my belt or come into a serious amount of money before I give it another shot.

Maybe I should be thankful to all the sports psychologists who gave me bad or unnecessarily dogmatic advice, because I would have never written this book if they hadn't. I am not a religious person and don't believe in destiny, but maybe this chapter of my life happened because I was meant to write this book, to shed light on my perspective of golf psychology. Regardless of how the world perceives my book, it is by far what I am most proud of at this point in my life.

Thanks for reading my book. I hope you enjoyed it!

There is no right or wrong,

Jason Burstyn

ACKNOWLEDGEMENTS

I would like to thank the people who helped me put this book together. To my very first proofreader who read multiple versions of the book and took the time to consult with me. Your advice was invaluable and helped me create a better story. Words can never express my gratitude.

I would like to thank my attorney, Thomas Julin, who reviewed parts of the book and clarified my legal questions.

I want to thank the University of Miami and the Richter Library for having so much great material that expedited my research and saved me countless hours of time.

I want to thank my cover artist, Luis Rondon for drawing a great cover and bringing my vision to reality.

I want to express my gratitude to the people who put me in contact with the professional golfers I interviewed throughout this book. I only had one direct contact: Erik Compton. For everyone else I had to work through a middle man. So to David Plati, Erik Compton, Craig Donoff and Carlos Velez, I truly appreciate your help with connecting me to these individuals.

I would like to acknowledge the people who agreed to do interviews. They did so out of the kindness of their hearts. They did not owe me anything and I can't express how much I appreciate it. Sometimes in life you just need a favor or a break, and I feel these people gave it to me. There were a lot of golfers who did not respond or said no despite the fact that we had close mutual connections. I have no hard feelings toward them; they do not know me and do not owe me anything.

From the bottom of my heart, I want to thank Erik Compton, Jonathon Kaye, Hale Irwin, Chip Beck, Bruce Fleisher, Gonzalo-Fernandez Castano, and Steve Jones. Without your interviews I would have never been able to write this book.

Originally, I wanted my book to be about the culturual differences between football and golf. But I realized it was going to be next to impossible to get the interviews I wanted. While I was at UM there was a Master of Business Administration program geared toward NFL players so there were a lot of NFL players walking around the business school. Being the hustler that I am, I approached a few of them in hopes of getting an interview. I interviewed one player, JT Thomas. Since it does not pertain to the book I decided not to share that interview, but I want to thank JT for taking the time to talk with me.

Since this book is anything but cliché, I am going to give my biggest thanks to myself. It took over three years to write this book, doing it on the side while I was in grad school and working. I wrote nearly every single letter, word, sentence, paragraph, and page in this book. Which is more than these shrinks—who need ghost writers and co-authors to write a majority of their books—can say. It wasn't easy for me to to admit the things I did and to express my opinions—which will hopefully get serious discussions started about the validity of golf psychology.

And lastly to the person who was with me every step of the way…

REFERENCES

Asselta, Ryan. "Rocco Mediate Talks Tiger Woods and the 2008 U.S. Open." GOLF.com, June 14, 2016. https://www.golf.com/tour-and-news/rocco-mediate-talks-tiger-woods-and-senior-pga-championship-win.

Baugh, Frank G. and Benjamin Jr., Ludy T. "Walter Miles, Pop Warner, B.C. Graves, and the Psychology of Football." *Journal of the History of the Behavioral Sciences* 42, no. 1 (2006): 3-18.

Belkin, David S., Gansneder, Bruce, Pickens, Morris, Rotella, Robert J., and Striegel, David. "Predictability and Stability of Professional Golf Association Tour Statistics." *Perceptual and Motor Skills* 78, no. 3 (1994): 1275-1280.

Broadie, Mark. *Every Shot Counts: Using the Revolutionary Strokes Gained Approach to Improve Your Golf Performance and Strategy.* New York: Gotham Books, 2014.

Cohn, Patrick, J., Rotella, Robert J., and Llyod, John. "Effects of a Cognitive-Behavioral Intervention on the Preshot Routine and Performance in Golf." *Sports Psychologist* 4, no. 1 (1990): 33-47.

Fannin, Jim. May 2011. "Golf in the Zone, Vol 1." Audio CD. Jim Fannin Brands, Inc.

Fannin, Jim. *The Pebble in the Shoe: 5 Steps to a Simple Confident Life.* Naperville: Simple Truths, 2013.

Ferguson, Doug. "PGA Tour Journey Sometimes Requires Long Rides, Cheap Motels." *PGA/Turner Sports Interactive*, January 16, 2016. https://www.pga.com/news/pga-tour/journey-pga-tour-sometimes-filled-long-car-rides-cheap-motels.

"How the PGA Tour and Web.com Tour reshuffle works," Golf News Net, September 22, 2017. https://thegolfnewsnet.com/golfnews-netteam/2017/09/22/how-pga-tour-web-com-tour-reshuffle-works-106972/

Jackson, Robin C. "The Preshot Routine: A Prerequisite for Successful Performance?" In *Optimizing Performance in Golf*, edited by P. R. Thomas, 279-288. Brisbane: Australian Academic Press, 2001.

Joyce, Nick and Baker, David B. "The Early Days of Sport Psychology." Monitor Psychology 39:7. 2008. http://www.apa.org/monitor/2008/07-08/sport-psych.aspx.

Mellalieu, Stephen D. and Hanton, Sheldon, eds. *Advances in Applied Sport Psychology*. Abingdon: Routledge, 2009.

Parent, Joseph. *Zen Golf: Mastering the Mental Game*. New York: Doubleday, 2002.

Perkins-Ceccato, N., Passmore, S. R., and Lee T. D. "Effects of Focus of Attention Depend on Golfers' Skill." *Journal of Sports Sciences* 21, no. 8 (2003): 593-600.

Rotella, Bob. *Golf is a Game of Confidence*. Contributions by Bob Cullen. New York: Simon & Schuster, 1996.

Rotella, Bob. *Golf is Not a Game of Perfect*. Contributions by Bob Cullen. New York: Simon & Schuster, 2007.
Rotella, Bob. *The Golfer's Mind*. New York: Free Press, 2004.

Rotella, Bob. *The Unstoppable Golfer: Trusting Your Mind & Your Short Game to Achieve Greatness*. Contributions by Bob Cullen. New York: Free Press, 2012.

Rotella, Bob. *Your 15ᵗʰ Club: The Inner Secret to Great Golf.* Contributions by Bob Cullen. New York: Free Press, 2008.

Ryba, Tatiana V., Stambulova, Natalia B., and Wrisberg, Craig A. "The Russian Origins of Sport Psychology: A Translation of an Early Work of A. C. Puni." *Journal of Applied Sport Psychology* 17, no. 2 (2005): 157-169.

Stangor, Charles. *Introduction to Psychology.* FlatWorld, 2014.

The School of Life. "Philosophy René Descartes." *YouTube.* Video File. September 11, 2015. https://www.youtube.com/watch?v=CAjWUrwvxs4.

Websites used to obtain information on scoring, results and prize money: www.pgatour.com, www.europeantour.com

Wertheimer, Michael. *A Brief History of Psychology*, 5ᵗʰ ed. New York: Psychology Press, 2011.

Wulf, Gabriele. "Attentional Focus and Motor Learning: A Review of 15 Years." *International Review of Sport and Exercise Psychology* 6, no. 1 (2012): 77-104.

Wulf, Gabriele and Su, Jiang. "An External Focus of Attention Enhances Golf Shot Accuracy in Beginners and Experts." *Research Quarterly for Exercise and Sport* 78, no. 4 (2007): 384-389.

Yancey, Allison, Czech, Daniel R., Joyner, Barry, Zwald, Drew, and Gentner, Noah. "The Experience of Preshot Routines among Professional Golfers: An Existential Phenomenological Investigation." *Journal of Excellence*, no. 14 (2011): 48-68.

ABOUT THE AUTHOR

AUTHOR JASON BURSTYN draws upon his experiences as a successful junior golfer, NCAA student-athlete, and regular on several professional mini tours to provide insight on what it's really like to "chase the dream" of a competitive golf career. With a specific focus on golf psychology, Jason sheds light on what he believes are serious flaws within the field. These flaws, he believes, ultimately prevent many golfers from reaching their full potential. Through his own on- and off-course stories, coupled with candid interviews with current and former PGA Tour players, Jason will leave you thinking differently about the cliché advice you may have recently heard at your local golf course or read in the latest-and-greatest golf psychology book.

CONNECT WITH THE AUTHOR

Please visit jasonbgolf.com

JASON BURSTYN

Made in the USA
Las Vegas, NV
21 November 2020